Bob & Hollis Koster

WEALTH
OR
MAMMON

Word & Spirit Institute NW
316 W. Young Street
Elma, WA 98541

RAY F. LANDERS

BETHLEHEM STAR PUBLICATIONS ™
P.O. BOX 85
NOKOMIS, IL 62075

Bethlehem Star Publications ™

Wealth or Mammon

by Ray F. Landers

Copyright © 1998 by Ray F. Landers

All rights reserved.

Printed in the United States of America.

International Standard Book Number 1-883654-08-4

To order books, tape series, or to set a date for a
seminar write or call:

Ray F. and Billie Sue Landers
World Ministries
5000 Dickey John Road Auburn, IL 62615
U.S.A.
Phone 1-217-438-3202

This book is lovingly dedicated
in the memory of a wonderful friend

Barbara Jean Oakley
April 9,1942 - November 23, 1996

One of the first directors of the Curse to Blessing seminars in the state of Illinois.
A long time friend who could rebuke me and
lovingly encourage me in the same breath.
Someone who continually patted me on the back
and would say.
"Where are the books, Ray?"

Contents

Chapter Three: Generational Curses......97

Chapter Four: The Spirit of Mammon......123

Acknowledgments

I owe a lot to my beautiful wife; she never gave up. She kept on going even when everything in the natural realm looked impossible and it looked like things would never change. She stayed by my side fighting the good fight of faith. God heard her prayers. Billie always knew there was a purpose in it all. She knew that God was forming a country boy into a man after His own heart. She could see what I could be instead of what I was. In the past, instead of seeking what was truly important in life, I was too busy trying to make millions. Without my precious wife, who is a true gift from God, this book would not exist.

I want to thank Don and Heather Aldous from Queensland, Australia. God used you to strengthen me during a critical time in my transition to do "God's business."

I could never have finished my first book without the help of some dear friends, Jim Kessler and his wife, Val. I appreciate the hours Jim spent praying, reading, researching, studying my notes, going to my seminars, and listening to the Spirit of God to help put this book on paper. No words can say, thank you, well enough. This man was truly a servant to me. He helped and encouraged me. He prayed for me. Jim ministers in the prophetic and is writing books of his own. Yet, God gave him the grace and patience to stop all to help me.

Jim Kessler, all I can say is God bless you and your household a 100-fold.

If you would like to know more about Jim and Val Kessler, you may reach them at: Full Life Ministries
317 South Oak
Nokomis, IL 62075 USA
Phone 1-217-563-7477

Introduction

The Art of the Deal

At a very young age I would go with my mother to every yard sale and auction there was. My mother was a professional. She was one of a kind, because she could buy and sell with an art. Mom had a gift that enabled her to talk to people, to negotiate, and to put a deal together. I loved to watch my mother. She would see something at a yard sale and if the price was marked at $10.00, she would bid them $1.00. The negotiations would begin.

She would see something that would be of possible interest to a person she knew and if the item was offered for $100.00, my mother would give a deposit to the seller and tell them that she would be back at a certain time. She also told them that if she wasn't, they could keep her deposit and sell it to someone else. Mother would then go to the person she thought she could sell the item to, and more times than not Mom would have their money, go pay the seller the rest of the price, and end up with a tidy profit. We would then put the article in the old pick-up and go deliver it.

Mom would make money and say, " Honey this is ours."

Then she would hold up a fistful of dollar bills. The $20.00, $50.00, and $100.00 bills were the ones I liked to feel and touch. At a young age I could not understand what money did, but I realized money had power. The more money you had the more power you had to buy and sell.

Many times I saw my mother eager to buy something and she would say, "I just don't have that much cash on me." Later, she would say, "I should have bought it, because I could have sold it for a profit!" So I realized to make money you had to have merchandise or money to do business. Money gives you the opportunity to take advantage of opportunities. It also helps you obtain the merchandise to sell for a profit.

I noticed when my mother bought she never allowed her emotions to get involved. She would not allow herself to become tied to things. Her emotions would not dictate the price she was willing to pay.

Mom would tell me, "If you pay too much for something you will not make a profit, Ray. You have to buy it right to sell it right. Never pay too much for something, honey, or you will be lucky to get your money back." Mom would always tell me a little profit is better than a piece of merchandise that you have too much money in.

Mother's rule was if you spent money, every dollar must have appreciation. It had to increase in value. Every dollar spent had to have a return. If you spent one dollar you needed to make two dollars, or at least a dollar and a quarter.

Many times I saw my mother trade. She would make a trade that would allow her 100% profit when sold. Several times I witnessed my mother selling things on credit. Mom would always tell me, "Ray, it is pretty easy to finance something when you have already made a profit."

It took me years to understand that when Mom financed things, she had no money in the item. She couldn't lose. I saw her make the purchasing price again plus interest.

Mom always told me that interest would kill you. It would put you into debt and never allow you out. The only one that won was the lender. Mom always told me the repayment of a loan was easy, but to repay the loan with interest only enslaves you.

You see my mother had a tremendous gift. She lived to function in that gift. She loved buying and selling. It really didn't matter what she bought or sold because her love was found in the art of the deal and the thrill of the process.

In other tapes and books I tell a lot of stories about my life, my father, my mother, and my family. It is easy for me to understand the importance of the first 84 months of a child's life. Ninety percent of life patterns are formed into a child by the age of seven. The other 10% is completed during the rest of their life. The first seven years of my life were with my mother going to auctions and sales. I was learning the art of listening, talking, and dealing with people.

The biggest asset a person can have in business is to listen to what people need. In business if you can fulfill a need and do it well, the financial rewards are very great. Most services that people perform in the professional realm are specialized. They learn to do one thing well and then watch the rewards of doing it. Financial rewards will always follow. Never do something half-hearted. If it is worth doing, do it fully.

Find Your Purpose

I had a friend who was a very successful auctioneer and real-estate broker, Bill. When my mother and I went to auctions most of the time Bill was the auctioneer. Bill would stop for a brief moment, see me and announce my name over the loud speaker: "Hello, Raymond. There's my boy!" It really made a little boy feel like someone important.

When he called me, Raymond, it was an inside joke because my mother did not like the name Raymond. Agitated, my mother would always say, " Bill, his name is not Raymond. It is Ray!" He called me Raymond to get my mother going. It never bothered me because I thought Bill Gaule was one of the greatest men on planet earth.

I owe him a debt of gratitude because he gave me some of the best advice I have ever received. One day he asked me a question I will never forget. He asked, " Raymond, what do you really want to do with your life? When you find that out, go for it with your whole heart and let someone else pay you for doing it."

I have sought to live my life with the guidance of those simple words. Bill had such an impact on my life that years later I named my first son, Willie, after him.

True or False

There are counterfeits in the body of Christ. There are flakes and fruitcakes in the body and I have seen them all. Counterfeits are teaching prosperity without the proper balance. They seem to say the right words while using the Bible, but something is wrong. Later in this book, you will see how some of these people are blinded to the ways of God's prosperity by the spirit of mammon.

Satan is a good counterfeiter. Satan is not a man in a black suit with red on the inside of his cape carrying a pitch fork. He is not Batman. He is an angel of light, and old Lucifer was the best - almost perfect. He was so good that he talked 1/3 of all the angels into committing treason against Almighty God. Satan is smooth. He is a master mind. He is a counterfeiter, and he tries to make it look perfect. Why do you think the U.S. Government made a new $100.00 bill. It sure wasn't because they thought it would be a good idea. The reason was simple. The counterfeiters had the $100.00 bill almost perfect. The enemy wants us to mistake his lie for truth. His sole objective is to disrupt and destroy our God given purpose and destiny.

I have learned a lot through the years, and when I teach on finance, it is not based on something I have read in a book or simply seen on television. It comes from years of studying the Bible. It comes from years in business fighting the competition, the banks, the lawyers, and the people who change their whole outlook on life when money becomes their god.

I know what it takes to be a husband and a father. I know what it is like to look at a pile of bills, and all the while, wondering how the money will come to meet all the obligations;

the banker, the insurance premiums, the real estate taxes, the unemployment taxes, the lawyers, and the accountants. I know the pressure of finances. I know how your mind can spin in circles wondering if you will go insane. I've experienced the inability to think straight because of the responsibilities and the failures.

I have been there and done that. Now, I know a better way. That is what I am going to teach you in the following pages of this book. You will see how the spirit of mammon controls nations, businesses, churches, families, and individual lives.

Through the grace of God you will find the freedom you have been seeking in this area of your life. Good reading and God bless!!

CHAPTER ONE

WEALTH OR MAMMON

Wealth or Mammon

MAT 6:24 States: *No man can serve two masters: for either he will hate the one, and love the other; or else he will hold to the one, and despise the other. Ye cannot serve God and mammon.*

This verse of scripture has been quoted many times in the church world. As far back as I can remember, I have been taught that mammon was money. Money, money, money, mammon was money. I would be told, " Ray Landers, if you love money you can't love God!"

Well boy, oh boy, that would blow the socks right off me. I could never figure out those old pastors who preached against "that filthy lucre", yet always cried for more "money." If you had money you were considered unholy, yet they'd cry continuously for more money. My head would spin.

I would say, "God, You gave me an ability to make money. It is Your gifting upon my life. Yet those in your body simply don't understand my calling. I can't understand why this spirit of poverty rules in your church."

Pastors magnified poverty by telling the saints this is how

God keeps them humble. Mothers would reach into their purses and children into their pockets to place change in the offering plate. I couldn't fully understand why, but my stomach would ache and I felt grieved in my spirit.

Believe me, one thing I fully understood, I did not want anything to do with that poverty mentality.

I had been taught all of my life that you could prosper by working hard and that with consistency came increase. I did not know a lot about God, but I did know enough to discern between being prosperous and being poverty stricken because of ignorance. I knew by watching my mother that you could do anything you put your mind to. She taught me to *shoot for the stars,* not to jump into a ditch of mud.

I believe with my whole heart that one of the most terrible deceptions that has invaded the church has come through the area of finances. The enemy has used the lack of understanding concerning the principles governing wealth and mammon to hold the children of God in bondage to a poverty mentality. Therefore, let's look into a few principles that explain wealth, and then move into the principles concerning mammon.

Principles of Wealth

In Deuteronomy 8:18, God says He will give us the power to make wealth. God would never enable us nor give us the power to do the opposite of His will. If He desires to empower us to make wealth, then wealth cannot be mammon. Mammon separates us from God and causes us to be double minded.

If wealth is not mammon, then it is very important for us to find the distinguishing characteristics that separate them. If we can separate wealth from mammon, then we can find the freedom to be empowered to receive wealth.

Normally during my seminars, I ask people to give me a definition of wealth. Most often they tell me wealth is money. Their answer serves only to put a smile on my face, for wealth is not money.

Wealth is land, houses, cattle, flocks, silver and gold bouillon. Wealth is anything in the land or above the land. Natural resources such as coal, iron ore, zinc, timber, and anything that the land has in or above it belongs to God. He controls it. God owns the cattle on a thousand hills. What are hills? What are cattle? They are wealth. God owns wealth. I understand money, and I understand wealth. The water belongs to God and the fish belong to God, but money is a product of this present world system.

Into whichever country I travel, I usually exchange my U.S. Currency for the currency of that country. It never fails. There is always an exchange rate between the two countries. Sometimes I laugh when I see the strange currency. It looks like funny money, play money. I often wonder if the money is real or fake. You see, money has no real power. It is only as powerful as the goods and services that it can purchase for us. Money is an inanimate object.

Each country has greater familiarity with their own money. If I laid out one hundred thousand dollars of Australian money on a table in the U.S.A. and said let's play monopoly, no one would think anything about it. They would think it was play money. Money is man-made, and the country that makes it establishes its value.

In America our money used to be backed by gold in Fort Knox. The debt in our country was secured by gold and silver. When I was a young man, all of our dollar bills were silver certificates (these could be redeemed at the bank for silver). All the coins were made out of silver and the pennies out of copper. In the 1960's our government decided we did not need gold to back our debts. We began using money printed by the Federal Reserve Bank to discharge our debts rather than actually paying them with secured currency. Our dollars are now called Federal Reserve notes rather than silver certificates.

Our country was the largest lender of money in the world until 1979. In 1980 we became a borrower and we went into a deficit position for the amount of one trillion dollars. By 1983 it was two trillion, and by 1996 it was 5.4 trillion dollars of debt.

In a business, a church, or a family, debt can consume you. Debt has the ability to destroy our nation. America cannot stand under this debt. Our country was built on godly principles. Take God out of our schools and out of or political system and we will not stand. Satan is a good counterfeiter. We need to know that this world's system of finance is not designed by God.

Many people have read the verse of scripture about the wealth of the wicked being stored up for the just. When I ask people the question," What is that wicked person's wealth?" Most of them will answer," Well, Mr. Landers, it is their money." Again, I just have to smile.

You see when you know the truth, the truth will set you free. Wealth is not money. A wicked person can have wealth, but when God is ready, look out. It will transfer to the righteous.

Look at the story about Jacob and his father–in–law, Laban. Ten times Laban changed Jacob's wages in 20 years, but God gave Jacob a dream about the spotted sheep and cattle. Jacob knew how to take advantage of an opportunity from the Lord. He made a deal with Laban that included the spotted livestock as a part of his wages. Before long Jacob owned more stock in the company than Laban. Sheep and cattle are wealth. God gave the wealth of Laban to Jacob through the transfer of cattle and sheep. Laban and his sons were angry with Jacob, but God commanded Laban saying, " Don't you dare harm him!" God can protect your health and your wealth.

When it is time for the wealth of the wicked to go to the righteous, I don't believe it will be through money. Yes, the money will be lost from that wicked person, but it will be in direct proportion to the loss of wealth. When God takes wealth away from a person, his money will soon depart.

In the world system, there can be a downward spiral. Let me explain. We sell true wealth (land, houses, cattle, flocks, silver and gold bouillon) to attain money. Money is what makes the world go round according to the world system. In other words, money is needed to buy and sell. When we sell wealth and replace it with money, we have the tendency to buy treasures and riches rather than invest in wealth. (Treasures are the things we fill our homes with that give us enjoyment or fulfill a certain purpose for our daily life-style.) When we buy treasures alone, our money loses value, because treasures wear out and depreciate in worth. Most of the world spends money for daily existence and for the treasures the world offers. Very few spend to attain riches and more importantly the wealth that God empowers us to receive.

Wealth has the potential to bring increase. Wealth will generate income. Income can be used to create more wealth, to buy riches or to buy treasures. When we fill our homes and lives with treasures, we show others and God where we have placed our heart. Riches, on the other hand, can deceive our heart and lead us away from God. Riches are the investments we make through the world system of finance. They can become our hope of security and salvation during rough times. This can cause our hearts to be stolen away from total dependency on God. We cannot trust in riches.

We must have an understanding of this present world system in order to make the wealth God desires us to receive. To understand this present system we need a clear grasp on the teachings of Jesus concerning mammon.

Principles of Mammon

There are four Scripture references given in the Word of God concerning the principles that govern and define mammon. All of them are found in the New Testament and each came directly from the teachings of Jesus.

A firm tie to Old Testament history exists through Jesus' use of the Chaldean word mammon. The Chaldean people where the rulers of the Babylonian Empire and their language was used to teach the secret arts of occult practices. A reference to these facts are found (Daniel 1:3-4) when Daniel was selected to be taught the language and ways of the Chaldeans during his Babylonian exile.

Jesus joins the nature of mammon directly to the old Babylonian system of commerce and worship. Remarkably, this same Chaldean word is used in each of the four Gospel scriptures. Therefore, the Chaldean meaning of the word mammon is very important in understanding what Jesus was teaching when referring to mammon.

The following is the *Strongs Concordance* reference to the word mammon; Greek 3126. mammonas, mam-mo-nas'; of Chald. or. (confidence, i.e. fig. wealth, personified); mammonas, i.e. avarice (deified):-mammon.

According to this reference mammon has two meanings; one is to personify wealth and the other is to deify wealth. First let us discuss the personalization of wealth and then flow directly into it's deification.

When the wealth of God becomes personified by man, it enters into the realm of human control and becomes mammon. Personalization of God's wealth by man causes man to believe he owns what God has created.

When man claims the wealth of God as his own, without godly influence, his wealth becomes mammon. Whenever man, in his fallen nature, tries to control the wealth of God, he creates his own system of finance.

In the beginning God delegated the use of the earth to man. He told Adam to be fruitful, multiply, and subdue the earth (Gen1:28). The word subdue means to place under complete authority. God gave man the delegated authority to bring the earth into man's subjection. He released the earth into the hands of man. All was well, until man disobeyed in the garden. After the fall, men began to misuse the authority God had given to him.

The gifts and callings of God are without repentance. Therefore, man had the ability to use the resources of the earth in a way that was contrary to the will of God. Since man was created with a free will, he has the ability to obey or reject the wisdom of God. God will always respect the will of each individual, even when their will goes against His will.

We must understand that man through his fallen state has created a system of wealth that does not find its roots in the wisdom nor counsel of God. Therefore, there are two systems of finance on the earth. Man's system where mammon can be found and God's system. Although the system man has developed is not centered in God's wisdom, God still gives respect to that system.

Once a group tried to trick Jesus concerning this truth. They asked him," Jesus, should we pay tribute to Caesar?" (Matt. 22:19-22.)

All my Christian life I have been taught that this scripture was pertaining only to taxation. Right? Not exactly! Let me show you a principle at work. When I do my financial seminars, I get a coin from the country I am in and ask the same question Jesus asked, "Whose inscription is on this coin?" I am usually given the name of a president or some other government dignitary. Jesus asked the question so others would understand by their own answer where the authority of the money rests.

When we take gold or silver, melt it into coin form and place a man or woman's inscription upon it, guess what? We have just transferred kingdoms. We have just made ourselves the authority and power controlling wealth. We take the gold and silver which is the true wealth of God and place it into a man-made system. We go into the world's kingdom. So Jesus said if it belongs to Caesar, give it to Caesar; but if it belongs to God give, it to God.

Jesus understood fully the tendency for humans to become tied to the object of wealth rather than the creator of wealth. That is why He said you cannot serve God and mammon. He was telling us that we cannot become slaves to this present system of finances. He wants us to decide with full understanding who has supreme authority over our lives, God or mammon. We cannot be servants to two masters!

More wars have been fought and lives sacrificed because of mammon than any other thing on this earth. Every nation has taken the wealth of God (land) and called it their own. When man wants to control what belongs to God, mammon becomes the governing principle and along with it comes the authority of man without the wisdom of God.

The personalization by man of God's wealth will always lead to the deification of wealth. The two go hand in hand. In times of old, men would go out into the forest and take a piece of wood and carve it into an image, overlay it with gold, bow down to it and give it worship. The wood and gold was God's wealth, yet they worshipped the image they formed as god.

They would convert true wealth into something unholy and worship it as a god. God does not accept nor control these practices. To the contrary, He judges them.

The kings of Babylon, the Caesars of Rome, and Hitler all deified themselves. They required the people who followed them to worship them as god, and why? Because they deceived themselves into believing they owned the wealth of God. The coming Anti-Christ will do the very same thing. He will set up an image of himself in the temple and require all mankind to bow in worship. He will be deceived by thinking he is control-ling the wealth of the world (remember no buying or selling will take place without his mark) (Rev.13:16-17).

Every human being has the ability to worship wealth. We must first serve God and give Him a principal role in our life. When we allow wealth to take the place of God, we will give the spirit of mammon a position of authority to guide our hearts. Therefore, we must understand that Jesus is not talking about riches alone. He is teaching about a spirit that attaches itself to those riches. The personalization and deification of wealth al-lows a spirit of mammon to enter the life of a person and deceive him. Mammon is a spirit, and it has distinct charac-teristics. Whenever there is a transfer from God's kingdom into this present system, the spirit of mammon has an interest in the transaction.

When Jesus told us we could not serve God and mam-mon, He was not talking about money, treasures, riches, or wealth alone. All of these things have no ability in themselves to be good or evil. Earthly possessions reveal the heart of man. The way we use our resources will determine their effect upon others and ourselves. We cannot allow ourselves to be controlled by mammon. We cannot become a slave to it. We are not called to serve mammon, but we were created to worship God.

The Lord teaches us that we should not despise mammon but understand the principles governing it and then walk wisely concerning its use. We must remember that mammon is God's wealth personified or deified by men. The following scripture will enlighten us to a balanced approach to mammon.

LUK. 16:9 *And I say unto you, Make to yourselves friends of the mammon of unrighteousness; that, when ye fail, they may receive you into everlasting habitations.*

In the above scripture, Jesus is telling us to be fond of mammon. Of course, He is not referring to the spirit of mammon, but to the wealth of God that men have made their own. In this scripture Jesus adds an adjective to the word mammon. He calls it the mammon of unrighteousness. Unrighteousness brings to our minds a vision of sinfulness and moral decay. It brings an aversion, a drawing back in horror, an instant repulsive reaction in each child of God.

None of us want to be unrighteous in the sight of God. For that very reason many have misunderstood the scriptures and their true meaning concerning mammon. Some Christians have conditioned themselves to believe that money is evil. But, when we refer to the Scripture, we learn that it is the love of money that is the root of all evil and not money (I Tim. 6:10). To love money above God is to worship money. When men make money the focal point of their desire, they inevitably lie, steal, and kill. That is why the love of money causes the greatest evils to be committed through the hearts and hands of man. Remember, who came to kill, steal and destroy? Satan! When men worship money they come under the influence of demonic control. On the other hand, if God has his proper place in your heart, money is only an object to be used for His glory. And then, the enemy has no door of opportunity to attack you.

There is a second meaning to the word unrighteousness. Unrighteousness is legal injustice. I believe Jesus was using this concept when teaching about mammon.

We all live with legal injustice. For the Christian, it is experienced on a daily basis. Each Christian can understand the existence of legal injustice when considering the laws concerning abortion. Abortion may be accepted by the law of the land, but it surely has nothing to do with acceptance according to the Laws of God.

In the same fashion, whenever a nation takes the wealth of God and uses it to create its own legal currency, legal injustice has taken place. Mammon has just been created. In this area, Jesus is calling us to understanding and not to aversion. He does not want us to draw away with distaste. This is signified by His injunction for us to make friends with mammon which is legal but unjust. He is saying it is not a sin to go into the world system of finance and to transfer its wealth into His Kingdom.

To make a friend, we must exercise agreement, find a common purpose, and make a commitment. Friendships are often used for purging uncleanliness and securing holiness.

To be fond of something is to hold it close in affection. We are to call mammon a friend and not a foe, because God is calling us to a higher understanding which is based on His wisdom and not just the wisdom of this present system of finance. When we use mammon wisely, we have the ability to place God's wealth back into His system for use in His Kingdom. Thus, Jesus states that when you fail (die) they may receive you into eternal habitations.

Our habitation and place of responsibility in His eternal Kingdom can be dependent upon how we use mammon. Mammon is found in the world system not in God's kingdom. Therefore, we always run the risk of attack from the enemy. Jesus is not telling us to run from mammon but to use it for His kingdom. In the process, we learn to overcome the spirit that seeks to attach itself to mammon. Thus, we become more mature in our responsibilities on earth and better trained for our future place in God's kingdom. This principle alone should alert us to the penalties of misuse and to the great potential of proper use. One thing I know is that the Lord is displeased with those who set on the sidelines and do nothing with the talents He gives.

LUK 16:11 *If therefore ye have not been faithful in the unrighteous mammon, who will commit to your trust the true riches?*

If we have not been trustworthy in the use of this world's system of finances, how can we gain the respect from our Lord and be able to oversee true wealth? His great desire for us is to understand what has taken place within this world and use that knowledge to gain wealth. He wants us to use mammon properly and become stronger than the spirit of mammon which seeks to destroy our lives. True faithfulness is found in following the principles and practices that Jesus teaches. Faithfulness is using mammon through the direction of the Holy Spirit while being careful to deny the spirit of mammon any control over our lives.

The Prodigal and Mammon

We have heard a lot about the prodigal son from the viewpoint of redemption, but lets look at him in reference to the spirit of mammon (Luke 15:11-32). The prodigal son is one of the best biblical examples concerning the transfer of wealth into the world's system and the attack that can come.

In this story, the youngest son went to his father and asked for his inheritance. When the father gave his son the inheritance, do you think he wrote a check for a million dollars and said here son, enjoy your inheritance and be blessed? No, the father gave his son cattle, flocks, and land. The word for goods in this text is the Greek word ousia (oo-see'-ah) which means property. The property was then sold by the young man before he went on his journey.

It is an amazing thing, but wealth cannot be controlled by the spirit of mammon. Wealth will continue to increase, but when wealth is sold and turned into cash, guess what happens? We are tempted to spend, spend, spend. If we are not careful, the money just burns a hole right in the center of our pockets and falls out. That spirit jumped off on the prodigal son and destruction entered in.

He went to a far country where no one knew him. He

began spending in riotous living. All the treasures of life could now be his. He became very popular in his new home, but he didn't have the maturity to handle money. When the money was gone, so were his newly found friends.

He probably made a few wise choices, yet on the whole, he soon found himself in debt. He really didn't have the means to live the new life-style he had created for himself. The spirit of mammon had deceived him into believing he had more than he did. This spirit will always give a false sense of security in order to bring destruction on us suddenly.

After time, he ended in debt without the ability to meet the obligations he had created. He fell behind in the payments and found himself in bankruptcy. He woke up one day without his inheritance and feeding the pigs. A Jewish boy who was forbidden to touch the carcass of a pig was so hungry, he was ready to eat the pig's food. He came to his senses and said, "My father's servants have it better than I do. I am going home."

When his father saw him, he ran to him and kissed him. The father ordered his servants to care for his son. One of them put sandals on his feet. Do you know why they put sandals on his feet? Servants always walked barefooted. His father said this is my son and not my servant. The father then put a ring on his finger and a robe on his back.

The son wept before his father and confessed he had sinned against him and heaven. Yes, the misuse of wealth is sin and places us in the need for repentance. When we misuse money we are hurting ourselves and our loved ones, and we need the forgiveness so freely given by our Heavenly Father.

The spirit of mammon is much stronger than the money it controls. Many of us have fallen into the same trap and need freedom. We need to come to our senses as the prodigal did and run to our Heavenly Father for the wisdom to use properly what He has placed within our hands.

True Life Stories

While living in the Midwest I have seen the spirit of mammon destroy many farm families. In one such family, grandpa farms with his son and the grandchildren receive the farm as an inheritance. One son wants to stay on the farm and work it. The other son wants to go to the city and get a job. The son in the city buys a new car and before long he wants to go into business for himself. He then goes to his dad to ask for money. His father gives him hundreds of thousands of dollars to put him into a business.

The young boy does not know anything about business and before you know it he is buried in debt. All the cash his dad had given him is gone and now he is about to be foreclosed on by the banks. He goes back to his father for more help and his father mortgages the farm to get the money to bail this son out of his problems.

The mistake in this is the money that his father gave him served only as a Band–Aid, it only covered a more severe problem. The son had a cancer and the Band–Aid could not cure the cancer. After a few years his son had to take bankruptcy anyway. The son had promised the father that he would repay the complete loan with interest.

The son had so much guilt that he was ashamed to go home. The son's mother wanted to see the grandchildren, yet the son couldn't face his parents. He was afraid of the rejection he could receive because of his business failure.

Now here is the other son. He stayed on the farm and has never asked his dad for anything. His wife had to go to work just to help make ends meet. One day here comes the other son and his family. Mom and dad are so happy to finally see the grandchildren they have a party that weekend. All the neighbors and friends come to see the son and his family. At the party, grandma gave the seldom seen son and his wife and their children all kinds of presents.

The son who stayed on the farm becomes terribly upset because of the gifts. His wife went to the kitchen in tears, crying because she had never received a present from grandma like the one given to her sister–in–law. His children could not understand why they didn't get any presents while their cousins where being loaded down with them. The faithful son left his father's home that day with his wife and children in complete disillusionment.

Arriving home, he and his wife stayed up all night discussing the different possibilities concerning his father's will. The next morning the son met with his father and asked him about the will. The father said, " Son, all I have is yours."

The son said, " Dad, I have never asked for anything and yet my brother has taken our family farm. Now every penny we make goes to the mortgage. My brother is home to stay and you let him move into your home."

The father loved both his sons and could not send one away because of his mistakes. One was paying the debt caused by the other and could not understand the forgiveness of his father toward his brother.

This true life story is much like that of the prodigal son. It is very clear how the spirit of mammon destroys relationships in families. This story is lived out in many families today. Whether there will be forgiveness and reconciliation will be dependent upon the commitment to Christ and not to personal feelings. The Father in Heaven is always interested in bringing healing to the areas where mammon has brought destruction.

I have seen and heard all kinds of stories on how destruction has come into families. Another story begins as a man is laid off from his job. A fellow worker in the same shop is also laid off and by chance they meet at the unemployment office.

While at the unemployment office, an old friend of the first man is also there and enters the conversation. The three of them are discussing general topics when the old friend asks the two if they would like to make some extra money.

The friend said,"My brother–in–law is building a new house and he needs the heating and air conditioning done. Can you two do it?"

Well, both of these guys were heating and air conditioning men and that is exactly what they did in the shop where they had just been laid off. They looked at each other with surprise and answered, "We sure can!"

They took the job and sure enough the two of them made out great. Word got around that these guys were moon lighting so they began getting all kinds of odd jobs. Their old shop still didn't have work, so the unemployment checks kept coming in. They were drawing these checks as well as making good money at the side work. Let me tell you, cash can sometimes make a man think crazy. Personal integrity can be lost over a dollar going into the pocket.

All of a sudden they found themselves working full-time just to keep up with the side work. The extra money they were receiving from the unemployment checks allowed them to undercut all the other heat and air contractors. They didn't have a problem with cash flow because they bid each job based on labor only, therefore the cost of the materials were the responsibility of the person to whom they gave the bid. This was working great until one of them looked into the actual cost of the equipment and saw how much more they could make if they furnished material and labor. On paper it looked great so they went to the bank and asked for a loan. The loan was denied because they didn't have a track record for repayment nor any tangible assets the banker could hang his hat on.

On Sunday one of these men went to his father's house for dinner. The father was retired and lived in a modest home. The house was paid for, plus the father had some savings in a local bank. The bank was the same bank where the partners had applied for a loan. During dinner the father asked his son about his wife and children and how work was going.

The father had worked at the same shop were his son had been laid off. Actually the father had gotten his son the job. The father still received his pension and insurance plan from the shop. The son told the father about the new work and how his partner and he were making very good money. He also mentioned that they would like to start their own business.

His dad thought that idea was wonderful. He started revealing to his son how he had had an opportunity to go into partnership with the original group which started the old shop. His wife had too much fear to allow him to enter into partnership. She felt it was safer to take wages rather than share the debt of a possible business failure.

The son told the father about a building over on the corner of 31st and Vine streets. He told his father that he and his partner wanted to rent it and start their own business. Well, good old dad got all fired up about the idea and told his son,"Let's go down to the bank in the morning and see the banker."

The banker told the father that they would love to help a new business, but they had to have security. Dad asked, "What do you need for security?"

The banker told him," I need something tangible."

The dad told him, " I have a savings account in your bank, and I own my own home without debt."

The banker said, " I feel sure your son will be able to succeed in business. If you want to start a business checking account with them the bank will loan you the money and put a mortgage against your home."

Dad said, " I think that will be fine."

When the father and son left the bank they were both smiling from ear to ear. The father told his son, " Don't say anything to your mother about this, because she hates debt. She would not be able to sleep at night with a mortgage on our home."

The banker got the mortgage and loan note ready and called the father. They said it was time for the paper work to be signed. Well, the happy day took place. The check was deposited into the business account and the business took off with great success. During the first few months of business, the two partners could not keep up with all the new work, so they hired men laid off from their old shop.

Before you know it, they hire office help and a manager. They thought they were making a lot of money because of all the contracts they were getting, but they were also responsible for all the unemployment insurance taxes, bonds, and interest payments. In the meantime, they each buy a new pick-up truck and jointly decide to buy two new work vans for the business. They didn't realize the amount of the payments going out to the banker. They were only aware of the gross dollars coming in and didn't realize the bottom line of the business.

One day the dad got a phone call. It was one of the owners of the old shop. The boss wanted to know if they could meet to drink a cup of coffee together. The dad accepted and the next morning they met at 9:00 a.m. at the local coffee shop. The old boss was a very concerned friend. He had always wanted the dad to be a part owner in his business.

Through the years this old friend had made a lot of wise investments and one of them was stock in the local bank. Gain-ing stock through the years, he had become a major stock-holder and he sat on the bank board. The information he had as a board member made it very difficult for him to talk to his friend, but as a friend he felt he must. He told the dad, " The bank is having a lot of problems with the loans we have made to your son and his partner. Bad checks are being written to suppliers. Furthermore, the bank has been notified by the government that they are going to levy the account for unpaid unemployment taxes. In the process they will freeze the account."

The dad could not believe his ears. The old friend told him that the bank was very concerned about their loans and that they were going to call in all the notes. The dad said, " I can't believe what has happened to them."

The old friend said, " In the old days we worked hard and borrowed very wisely. We did without and grew our business on solid foundations. Your son and his partner were good workers but they had no knowledge of business. They hired way too much help and hired an office manager and clerical help which took more money than they could make. What I am really uneasy about is your home. We have a mortgage on it and the bank has always considered you as one of the customers that made our bank what it is today. The foundation of our bank has been the hard working men and women like you, who have saved all their life for retirement."

The old friend continued, " What really hurts me is we gave you an 80% loan on your home. With the interest and late charges I am afraid there is no equity left. If we call the note, your house could go into foreclosure."

The dad was speechless. He looked at his old friend and asked, " What can I do? What is my wife going to say and do?" He pleaded with his old friend and asked him, " Please send nothing to my residence that might alarm my wife to the indebtedness on our property."

His old friend said, " I will do the best I can but I am just one board member with only one vote. The new board members don't know the old people and the old ways of honor. All they look at is the profit or loss of the bank. The bottom line is all that matters." The meeting ended and the two old friends parted with pain and grief in their hearts over the circumstances at hand.

The dad drove all over town trying to find his son. When he finally found him, the son could not look his dad in the eyes. His dad was so upset that an argument started over the circumstances, and they both said a lot of words neither one really meant to say. The father's blood pressure went sky high, and when he left his son, it felt as if his heart was going to explode.

When the father pulled the car into his driveway, he passed out and fell toward the steering wheel. He landed against the wheel in such a way causing the horn to blow. The Mother heard the horn and came running to the vehicle. After seeing her husband bent over the steering wheel, she ran into the house and called 911. Frantically she said," I believe my husband has had a heart attack."

Within minutes the ambulance was there with the paramedics. They rushed him into the emergency room of the hospital. The Dad had a massive heart attack and stroke.

The son found out within the hour and rushed to the hospital. His mother and sister were already there crying their eyes out. He listened as they related to him the recent events concerning his father. He didn't have the heart to tell his mother and sister about the argument with his father.

His mom was a basket case. She was a person filled with fear and doubt. She normally saw the worst. Mom kept saying, " How am I going to make it if your dad dies? I need his retirement money and social security just to live. Oh, if Dad dies what am I going to do?"

The son stayed with his mother and sister all night until the early hours of the morning. Around 4:00 a.m. the doctors came out to the family and advised them that the dad had died. Mom collapses and the sister folds up into her brother's arms. The son can't believe what he is now experiencing. Within hours of the death, the family has to make funeral arrangements. The funeral director was very kind and helpful, and the day of the funeral comes and goes.

Weeks pass by. One day the mother gets her mail. The mailman request her to sign for a certified letter. In opening the letter she finds out that the bank was demanding full loan payment. If the money was not in the hands of the bank within thirty days they were going to start the legal proceedings to foreclose on the property. The same day the son receives notices from the bank on all their loans. The manager and the office help could not keep it to themselves. Everyone knew within the day that the bank was foreclosing.

There was a desperate need for the son and his partner to pull together assets for the life of the business. His partner also had problems at home. The wife was having an affair with a man that worked in the old shop. The partner had financial obligations from his wife's use of credit cards. The partner said that his wife and children were out of control and he knew there would be a divorce.

The son went home and his wife was weeping uncontrollably. The children were crying because mom was crying. The phone rings. He answers it and on the other end he hears the voice of his mother. She is hysterical about the notice she had gotten in the mail. He doesn't know what to do or say.

The next day he went to his mother's home. When he arrives, his sister is present with her husband. Well, you guessed it. The son can't bear his mother's pain. She has all the bills laid out on the kitchen table. The hospital bill, the funeral bill, every utility bill, and all the expenses. She also had every savings account, life insurance policy, every penny she knows about accounted for in the paper work. In the midst of tears she says, " The medical bills will take most of my small savings. The insurance barely pays the funeral bill. The money I have in checking will pay the utilities for this month. But what am I to do for the future?"

The son is sick. The sister says to her brother, " How much money do you have and when will you be able to pay this mortgage off at the bank?"

The son explains," I don't have any money, even the truck that is parked outside will be repossessed by the bank."

At that time the brother–in–law blows up like a big bull, " What do you mean there is no money? How in the world could you spend all of that money your dad gave you?" The brother was speechless.

The mother is hopelessly crying," I'll be on relief from the government and in government housing."

All of this is more than her son can handle. He leaves the house in tears, blaming himself for his father's death and the loss of all the money.

When he gets home the wife is worse than before. Her mother and father had called and told her, " We told you not to marry him. Now look at this fine mess you are in. The whole town knows you are broke and being foreclosed on. Do you know how many phone calls we have had today about that deadbeat husband of yours?"

The son cannot stand the pressures of life. That night he goes out and gets totally drunk. When he comes home he drives his pick-up into the garage and hits his automatic garage door opener to close the garage door. Being as drunk as he was he fell asleep in the truck with the motor running. He was found by his children the next morning in the pick-up. The motor was still running, the carbon monoxide from the exhaust had killed him. The whole town believes he killed himself. No one believes it was an accident.

The ending of this true story is a very sad one. The mother lost her home and had to go on state-aid and welfare. She did have to move into a government housing complex. She only lived a few years. The mom died of a broken heart caused by the loss of her husband and son. She had more faith in unbelief than she ever had in success.

The father died in vain. He always dreamt of being part owner of the old shop. The sense of loss and need to own a business destroyed the father because he tried to see his vision accomplished through his son. The father was only a laborer. He wasn't a business man. His son was never trained to run a business.

The son not only destroyed his life but left a lasting impact upon his children. All they will remember is seeing their father dead in a pick-up truck with everyone insisting it was suicide. The wife will wonder if she is being punished for marrying her husband without her parent's consent.

The sister is a basket case. She lost her father, mother, and brother. There is no inheritance left to her. She begins walking in the same fear her mother always had. She cannot forgive her husband for the harsh words that were spoken to her brother the day he died. Her husband doesn't know how to minister healing to his wife and lives his life with a marriage full of pain and stress.

Do you see how the spirit of mammon absolutely destroyed this whole family. Fear and greed are both open doors for the spirit of mammon to destroy and kill. We must fight the good fight of faith and not run from mammon, but face the problems it can cause fearlessly. God has called us to be overcomers in this life not paupers. We can see the evil afar off and with God's help protect ourselves from its power.

I would like to pray with you concerning the power of this spirit in your life. Parts of this prayer may not apply to your situation, but please receive from the Lord what He would desire you to receive. Please speak the prayer out loud, so your confession may be established with your own lips.

Prayer:

Dear Father, I renounce the ability of the spirit of mammon to continue it's work in my life.

I now see the difference between what You control and what the enemy tries to control through this world system.

Please give me wisdom and protection as I seek Your will in my life concerning the use of unrighteous mammon.

Please heal me and any members of my family that have been injured by this spirit.

This spirit must leave me and my dealings with money. I give all I have to You my Heavenly Father. Teach me Your ways that I might attain the wealth You desire.

Fill my life with Your Spirit of Wisdom where mammon once dwelt. I ask all this in the name of Your precious Son, Jesus Christ. Amen.

Notes

CHAPTER TWO

FREEDOM TO PROSPER

Freedom to Prosper

Duet. 8:18 states that the Lord gives us the power to make wealth. God's wisdom is the power to make wealth. God wants you to have the wisdom or practical insights into the realm of finances so you can live a productive life. He wants you to feel secure in your search for His will in this area. It is His will for you to make a friend of riches, rather than becoming a slave to them. The following parables have the ability to give us insight concerning the truth about making wealth.

In Matthew 25:14-29 there is a parable about the talents. The master called his servants together to entrust them with his possessions and talents according to their ability. To the first he gave five talents, and to the second he gave two, and to the third he gave one. The goods he gave them were merchandise and the talents money.

The scripture says that the servant with five immediately went to work trading. The servant with two talents did the same, but the servant with one talent hid it. When the master came home he wanted an account of their funds.

The one with five said, "Master, I have been entrusted with five talents. Behold here is another five talents."

The master was very pleased and said. " Well done."

The one with two talents came to the master with the same report he said," Master, you gave me two talents. Behold I have made two more."

The master was well pleased and said, " Well done, you good and faithful servant."

Now the one that had only one talent buried it, and the master was very upset with him. This servant was told he could have at least given it to the money exchangers and gotten usury (interest) on the money. The one with the five talents received this man's talent.

In this parable, all the profit came by buying and selling. Through trading, increase came. My mother always bought and sold, and when I read this I can see my mother as the master and me as a servant. The deals my mother made seemed to always bring increase, so I could not understand why anyone would ever bury a talent. Was it fear of failure, fear of himself, or fear of his master?

The master gave each one according to his ability. He knew the weakness of each servant, yet entrusted a talent to them. The problem did not rest with the trusting master, but with the distrusting servant. The others knew the kindness of the master to entrust them, but this servant saw his talent as a means for the master to judge him. He misjudged his master and received the very judgment of his own heart.

Should we look at our lives in the same way as the distrusting servant? Unfortunately some of us have. It is possible that we have been taught by well meaning friends or church leaders to feel exactly that way. We may have been told that riches only cause headaches and trouble. This type of thinking will cause us to misuse what the master has placed within our hands. It will be impossible for us to use what we have to its fullest potential. We will not use the very things God has given us to help establish His kingdom.

Percentage or Multiplication

This parable also speaks of the master's desire for us to gain wealth through multiplication. The least return we can get on our money is interest from the banker. It is a safe return, but a very poor return. Most bankers will make more money with what you give them than you will.

God works through multiplication not percentages. If you place one kernel of corn in the ground, you will receive hundreds if not thousands of kernels in return. If you had ten cows and each had a calf the first year, you would have doubled your investment. You would never imagine one-tenth of a calf per year. Yet, when we look at our money, we are happy to receive ten percent per year increase. That is not God's way of increase. This parable tells us the master is well pleased when we make increase as He makes increase.

Occupy until I Come

Another parable is found in Luke 19:12-27. In this parable there were 10 servants and each of them receive a pound a piece. The master said to them," Occupy until I come."

When I do my financial seminars, we occupy a building and thousands of people show up. In military terms, when we occupy an area we make it safe. We take an area and we occupy it. When you study this out in the Greek, the word occupy means to do commerce, to do business - to buy and sell. When the master said, " Occupy until I come," he didn't mean for us to set in one place and fold our hands. He meant get out there and trade. He has commanded us to do well in business.

The master on his return from securing the kingdom wanted an account from his servants. The first bondservant received one pound and by trading he turned it into ten pounds. The master was so pleased that he gave him ten cities to oversee. The second servant had one pound and turned it into five pounds. The master gave this servant five cities to oversee. The third servant hid the pound in the ground and did nothing with it. The master was furious with this servant, took away the one pound, and gave it to the servant that was the best qualified to use it properly.

When I talk to people they ask me the question," How do you make money, Mr. Landers?" I tell them these two parable and explain to them that all increase comes by buying and selling. The Lord gives us the ability to make wealth by multiplication and not by percentage. You must secure wealth with your increase.

Whenever you exchange wealth for money, the enemy is right there with the spirit of mammon to tempt you into a mistake. Satan is a master deceiver. There is nothing new under the sun except you and me. We must be taught his schemes and be wise in the affairs of finance.

While teaching His disciples Jesus told wonderful stories. You know I love to tell stories. I teach all over the world, and when I come back into an area, the people will say, " Oh, Mr. Landers, that story you told in your last seminar I will never forget."

A friend of mine once told me," Ray, if you are a good teacher you will know because people will not forget. If you see a traveling evangelist or teacher and you can't remember what he taught on, it must not have made an impression on you."

I have been to many places and have heard many great sermons, but the ones I really remember are those that are tied to a life story. Those are the ones I never forget. I like to hear about the business men who have lost everything, but through the hand of God everything is restored with more added.

Diligence in Business

I have seen one of the best businessmen go down to bankruptcy because he wasn't diligent. In business he was sharp. He knew the markets. He knew where every penny was and the heart beat of his business. His wife got saved and filled with the Holy Spirit, so the husband starts going to church. A wonderful thing happens, he gives his life to the Lord.

At first everything is wonderful. The business man stands up in church and testifies how God has helped him with a big contract and how much money they made. For the first year this man is witnessing and telling everybody how God is his partner in his business. Before you know it, everyone wants him to come to their church and give his testimony. He goes to the full-gospel businessmen's meetings and gives his testimony.

Over the next several months he is on the move. His calender is full with speaking engagements. Yet, he has not been tested as a Christian. He has not gone through the wars. This man is a baby Christian. Remember one thing, when you are in the Lord's army, sooner or later your war will begin. Your faith will be tested. You will be proven before the fullness of the promise is realized.

This man stopped running his own business. In order to keep the new speaking engagements, he decided to hire an office manager. Because of the plans before him, he could easily justify the expense. The manager needed a secretary, and there went more money.

This man had made tremendous money in his business. The money was made because he caused it to happen. He looked at every situation and watched every penny spent.

Whenever you give up your position and hire a manager, you don't have to be a rocket scientist to figure out increase in labor costs cuts profit. No manager will ever run your business as you would. Money is not spent the way you would spend, therefore you must keep a close watch. The old boss would buy used at 10 cents on the dollar, but the manager begins to buy everything new, and money starts flying out the window.

Now comes the attack of the enemy. This new Christian is still on milk. He hasn't eaten any meat. His faith has not been tested. The enemy begins to launch a full attack.

After a period of time, the man returns to check on his business. He finds out that the manager and the secretary have taken hundreds of thousands of dollars. The two of them had masterminded a way to take the funds. They had also charged a very large amount of building materials to his accounts. He also found that they had not paid the payroll taxes, and the taxes were going to collection. Within days the state had frozen all his checking and saving accounts.

Immediately, the unemployment office comes in to do an audit. While doing the audit they found that he had hired all kinds of independent contractors to do work, but paid them by the hour. Every check had the job number and the hours worked by the dollar amount per hour. With that on each check, the paper trail was easy for the audit. Now each dollar that was spent was subject to all federal, state, and unemployment tax.

He was also liable for workmans compensation insurance. He had always paid his premiums in advance and at the end of the year an audit was done to see if there was a credit or debit. When the insurance company did the audit, it picked up that most workers were paid by the hour instead of by the job. On top of this a man had fallen to his death from improperly installed scaffolding. There was no compensation insurance on this particular project, because his manager allowed the man to bid the project, and then paid him by the hour.

This man's business was set up as a corporation. He was the president and his wife was the secretary. Any corporate officer is always liable for any federal or state tax. Immediately the state filed liens against all personal and corporate assets. The worst happened when all personal checking and savings accounts were frozen. Corporate and personal checks were bouncing like red rubber balls everywhere.

This man had entered a life and death struggle. He had entered the fight of faith. He was one of the finest and sharpest business men in the area. Now he was the talk of the town. This fight would be the biggest fight he had ever had. If he wins, his faith will be even stronger; if he loses, satan would destroy him.

The first test was the taxes. He went to his old banker to get help. The banker told him he could not make the loan without board approval. The first Thursday of every month was the board meeting. That night the banker presented the man's request and a way of repayment for the loan.

The board was an old group of business men and local farmers that had lived in this community all of their lives. One board member said, " We need to help him get out of this time of trouble."

Another board member agreed and said," Yes, he has been a great customer and has had some big loans here. His savings have been quite substantial through the years."

One of the most successful men in the area was very wise and listened to everyone. After they all gave their nickels worth, they asked him what he thought. He said, " I have listened to all of you and I want to ask you a question. How could such a good businessman get so slothful in business? Another thing

I don't understand is how could a man have so much cash in our bank in CD's, savings, and checking, and end up without it. Did he not know what was going on? Could he not see the manager and the secretary taking all of his cash out of our bank? Another thing I know for a fact, he would never write a check if he did not have the money in his account. Look at how many months his checking account has been in an overdraft position. Why did he not have his taxes paid on the employees? Why is he traveling all over the countryside weeks at a time and not tending to his own business? I just can't understand how a man as smart as he became so dumb. Would you really loan this man money? I must tell everyone of you that I would not give him a dime until I knew his whole financial picture. What we are looking at tonight may only be the beginning of the true picture of this man's problems."

With those words spoken, the entire board went from helping him to the same opinion of the older man. The board voted no to the loan request. However, they told the banker to tell him that if he could give them a true picture of his finances, that they would look at it next month.

The next morning at 9:00 a.m. the businessman went to the bank to see the banker. He walked behind closed doors, and sat in the chair that faced the front of the banker's large desk. The banker looking him straight in the eyes said, " Your loan has been denied."

He could not believe his ears. In total shock he said," I can't understand it! Why? I have never been turned down at this bank in my life. What happened? Why was I turned down?"

The banker looked at him with all honesty and said," Because you were slothful in business. You were not tending to your business. You were running all over the countryside and not tending to your own business."

The business man was caught totally of guard and said, "Oh, but I hired a manager to help in the office."

The banker looked at his clock and said," I am sorry. I don't want to be rude, but I have another engagement outside the bank this morning. The board told me last night to tell you to get all your numbers together and have them ready for the next board meeting."

The business man felt that the banker was saying by his actions, " Don't you understand, I am the boss? Even though I have employees, the buck stops here. Right here. Don't you understand? You cannot blame everyone in town for your problem. The problem is this, you did not tend to business!"

He left the bank with his head spinning. The enemy was driving him crazy with fear and doubt. His own wife went against him the moment he got home. His children were falling apart. The kids at school had been harassing them about their dad's problems. How many of you know that kids can be ruthless? Their tongues are sharp and vicious.

His children had never seen bad times. All they knew was that home was their home and everything they needed was always there. Dad had always been a great provider and mom was the best cook and housewife. The house was always perfect.

This woman had come from a very wealthy family. She

was her father's little girl and was given anything a youngster could desire. When she married, her husband followed the same tradition and gave her anything she wanted. When her grandmother died, the inheritance she received gave her the opportunity to build her dream home. Her friends had not shared in the joy of her being able to have a nice home. They envied her and always wanted something better for themselves.

Mom was scared. All of her friends had called her that day. The gossip around town was getting completely out of hand. She was a very prominent lady in the community. All of her friends were in competition with one another trying to stay ahead of the Jones'. All of these friends were consumed by the spirit of mammon.

Well, how many of you know people's tongues love to wag when the juiciest story is unfolding? The stories were growing out of proportion. Her friends' husbands were all businessmen in the community. One of her girlfriends had a father on the bank board. He leaked the information to the girlfriend's husband. You can imagine how quickly the phones rang when her friend's husband told his wife the news. The girlfriend couldn't wait to tell everyone she knew. She also added a few more points to make the story even juicier.

This wife's so called friends began calling. They acted concerned for her, but started telling her of all the stories that were going around town. One called and said,"We are sure that your husband will land in jail."

Another called and said, " Dear, you need to protect interests. I have a name of a good attorney for you."

By the time her husband got home, the devil had tormented her out of her mind. The husband was speechless. They had such a wonderful marriage without one serious disagreement. The fear of failure, the fear of lack, and the fear of disaster had entered into both of them. That night was a nightmare. For the first time in their marriage, he slept on the couch.

The next morning he was up before the sun. He went into the coffee shop and all the old gang was there. One of the men at the table had his back to him, but the other men were looking straight at him. The closer he came to the table, the more he realized that the topic for the morning was his situation. The man whose back was to him was doing all the talking. The funny thing about it was that he did not even know this man. Well, you could cut the air with a knife. The businessman extended his hand to meet the man speaking. This man became as speechless as the other men at the table. One by one everyone seated at the table left the coffee shop. The man looked around the cafe. Every eye in the cafe was on him.

He slowly sipped on a cup of coffee and thought to himself, how could I have been so stupid. For years this cafe was the place I ate breakfast, signed contracts, and brought customers. Today I was the topic of breakfast. His thoughts turned to prayer and he said, " Lord, what am I going to do? I don't have enough money to buy this cup of coffee. My pick-up is out of gas. My kids need money. My wife needs household money. Lord, what am I to do?"

He went into his office and closed the door. Burying his head in his hands, tears pouring down his face, he said, " Lord, I don't know what to do. All my assets are frozen. I have no cash. My utilities are ready to be shut off, and Friday I owe all of my employees their wages, but I have no way to pay them."

Within a few minutes he heard doors opening, cars and pick-ups were coming into the parking lot. The men went about their normal routine and one of them said, " Hey, the real boss is here."

Most of the employees had been with him for years, so they were loyal workers. He came out of the office and said, " Men, I need to talk with you."

The men got chairs and grabbed a cup of coffee and said, " Okay, boss. What is going on and how can we help?"

Well, those words were the most encouraging words he had heard in days. He said, "Men, you have all been faithful employees and this business has always been good to all of us. Now I am in a mess. It is my own fault, but I didn't realized that my own business was being run down hill so fast. I should never have allowed the manager and secretary so much authority. My cash is gone. The payroll taxes are not paid. The state and federal taxes are not paid, and the government has frozen all my assets and bank accounts. I am being sued for an accident where a man fell off scaffolding to his death. I don't even know if I have any insurance to cover the accident. The utilities are ready to be shut off, and the bank denied my loan. So as I am speaking to you, I have no way of paying any of you this week."

All the men looked around the room at each other and one man stood up. He asked, " Boss, can I speak for the men?"

The boss said, " You certainly can."

He replied," Well, the boys and I have been talking and we knew for a long time things were not right, but didn't know where you stood. The manager was no manager and we all knew it. We have no idea how much money has been stolen, but we know you and we all want to help if we can. There is plenty of work right now, so we thought we could all keep working and see if we could lease, buy, or work something out with you until you get your feet back on the ground. We have all counted the cost of what we thought it would take for the insurance and utilities plus the miscellaneous expenses. We think we can generate enough income to keep things going. You still have all the equipment, so we thought we could go to the bank and sign the notes and pay the payments for you. We would make an agreement to let you have everything back as soon as you are able. We believe in each other and most of all, boss, we believe in you."

With tears pouring down his face, he thanked them all and told the men, " I really appreciate what each of you are willing to do. Please let me think about it tonight. Tomorrow I'll give you an answer."

As the men left the shop to go to their jobs, he went back into the office and started going through the books. The phone started ringing. His creditors were demanding their money and making threats. His guts started churning and turning and he felt very nauseous. The more he looked at the books, the sicker he got. Hundreds of thousands of dollars were stolen. All the cash that he had worked a lifetime to build was gone. He could not believe all the bills that were unpaid. He quickly got the computer going and started doing an accounts receivable and an accounts payable list. By the end of the day, fear had taken its toll on him. How many of you know that fear will not pay any bills? When you make any decision in fear, it is the wrong decision! Fear was choking the life out of him.

He went home late that night and his wife was on the phone. He could hear her saying, " Mom, I don't know what happened. I don't know how much money we need... Mom, cut it out. He is a good husband and father. He has always been a great provider. He has always loved me and been faithful to me and besides that he loves the Lord."

While hearing this conversation he knew his wife had no idea he was home. He went back into the garage and closed the door. Here lately he had been doing a lot of praying and crying, " Lord, help me, show me what to do." When he had quit crying he went back into the house saying, " Honey, honey, where are you?"

He heard his wife saying, " Mom, I have to go. I have got to get off the phone. Mom, I love you. Good-bye."

He went over to his wife, gave her a big kiss and a hug and told her he loved her. Tears came to her eyes and she just buried her face into his chest and wept. That night was a night the two of them will never forget. God spoke to their hearts and told them, " You need to trust Me, I will be there for you! Do not to forsake each other, but stand as one."

The next day the boss called another meeting and told the men that they could make the arrangements to take over the business. He went to an old high school buddy who was an attorney. He told him that he was in big trouble and needed legal help. He explained to him that all of his money was gone and that the state and federal government had frozen his accounts. Within hours the attorney was at work making phone calls and getting the information he needed.

The attorney found out the house was not in his friend's name, but actually the land was in his father-in-law's name. The grandmother had died and left an inheritance to his wife. The wife built her house on a wooded area which was adjacent to a lake. Her father had always owned the land and when she built the house, her father told her to go anywhere on the property and build her dream home.

The father had not deeded the property to them, but it was in his will for her to receive the entire timber at his death. The attorney called them that night and said, " I have some good news. Your house is safe. Your father–in–law still has title to the land which goes back to his father. So no court of law can take your home from you." When they heard that news they rejoiced. Both of them thanked God.

Within a few days the men had gone to the local bank and given all the information to the banker. The night of the board meeting rolled around, and the board voted yes to their loan request. The next morning the banker called the shop and told all of them that they had gotten their loan.

Within hours the attorney calls and says, " Do you know your shop is in a land trust?"

The business man replied, " Oh yes, I do. When I bought this property the man I bought it from had the land trust for his children. So he sold me the property and we just took over the land trust at the bank."

The attorney told him, " You must assign your beneficial interest to someone or sell the property immediately."

That night when the men came in he asked them if they would consider buying the real-estate. One of the men said,"Well, boss, how much is it?"

The price of the property was established and this man agreed to loan the group the money out of his own savings. Furthermore, they made an agreement with the boss that they would give him a check every week, just to keep things going like old times. The boss agreed and accepted the pay.

Next was the audit on the payroll taxes. When the auditor came he was from the pits of hell itself. Immediately he made life miserable. The next few weeks were terrible. After the auditor left, the businessman's attorney said, " We are in big trouble. Every check has in the memo the job number and the hours worked times the dollar amount per hour. All of these men are employees. Your secretary was very efficient, but anytime you pay a man by the hour he is your employee. An independent contractor works by the job, and he gives you a bill on the bid. I don't know how to beat this. This is going to be a tough one."

Within weeks the attorney received the papers for the lawsuit concerning the man that had fallen to his death. The attorney found out there was no insurance on the job. With two strikes against his friend, the attorney advised him, " It does not look good. You may be sued and forced into bankruptcy. One thing you must realize is that even if you take bankruptcy the federal and state liens will not go away. You will carry them to your grave."

Within the month, the attorney got the bad news on the tax audit. With penalties and interest it was over a quarter of a million dollars. The attorney gasped at the figure. He knew it was bad, but he never dreamed it could be that bad. He called his friend with the bad news. There was a pause on the phone and his friend said, " Are you sure?"

The attorney replied, " Yes, I am sure, and the only thing that makes it worse is that your wife is also liable. She is a corporate officer."

That night the businessman went home and told his wife the horrible news. All they could do was shake their heads in disbelief. They held hands and starting praying and said," God, we are trusting You. We don't know what to do, but we are trusting in You."

One day the bank called the house and told them that the unemployment people were at the bank and had an order to disburse any funds they had in the bank. They asked," They already have all our money. What else could they take?"

The bank told them," They are going to seize your children's college fund. We know it belongs to your children, but since your social security numbers are on the account, the government has a legal right to take the money."

They couldn't believe their ears. A lifetime of savings for the children's education was gone. They hung up from the bank and called their attorney. Sure enough the attorney told them the same thing. He said," I asked you specifically about money and you told me you did not have any money."

Both of them said," We have had this savings since our children were born. It was always their money."

The attorney said, " I am sorry. If you would have told me about the money, I could have told you exactly what to do, but now it is gone."

The two of them were sick. Again they prayed, " What about the education of our children, Lord? What are we going to do? Every time we turn around we are attacked."

Months turned into a year and then another year, and the pressure just kept growing. One day the attorney was going through some folders, and he noticed a letter from the Secretary of State. It stated that the yearly fees had not been paid for the corporate tax. Being a Saturday there was no way of getting in touch with the corporate tax department to check out his hunch. Monday morning the attorney had to be in court at 9:00 a.m.

When he left the courthouse, he walked over to the elevator and went down to the 4th floor. Going to the corporate tax office, he asked the status of the corporation of his friend.

" Well," the secretary said, " You can have that name if you would like."

The attorney looked puzzled. He said," I beg your pardon. I don't understand what you mean by your statement."

" Oh," she said," The tax hasn't been paid in over five years."

The attorney asked, "Are you sure about all this?"

The woman looked at the computer screen and said," I am positive. This tax has not been paid in five years."

The attorney asked, " What does that mean to the state?"

" To us they are out of business and after 18 months anyone who would want that name for a corporation could have it," was her reply.

The attorney asked, " Is that your policy?"

The secretary said, " Oh, yes. Our policy is that after 18 months we count them as a dead corporation."

The attorney smiled from ear to ear and said to himself, this is going to be a good day. He went back to his law office and started digging. The statutes he wanted showed him that the corporation was not a valid corporation, and since it wasn't valid, his friends were not corporate officers and not liable for the tax personally. He knew it was going to be a fight, but it was a fight on solid ground.

That weekend he took his old friend and his wife out for dinner. After dinner he said," Are you ready to hear some good news?" The couple looked at each other and stared at the attorney. He said, " I think your manager and secretary forgot to pay a bill."

They said, " Well, what is so good about that."

The attorney laughed and said," Well, they forgot to pay

the corporate tax which was to be paid yearly. If the tax was not paid in 18 months, you were no longer a valid corporation in the state. For five years your corporation has been legally out of business. With this we are going to show the state and the federal government you are not personally liable for those unemployment taxes. It will be a fight, but I believe we can win."

Well, the fight began and, oh, what a war. How many of you know that when you go through wars someone always gets hurt or killed, mentally and physically? The wife and kids got hurt mentally. They tried to stand in faith and believe God for a miracle, but their faith got weaker day after day, week after week, year after year. The years flew past, and before you know it the kids were graduating from high school. Their softened hearts of youth had became hardened by the years of turmoil. They didn't want to hear anything about going to church or God. Their reply was always," If God is there all the time, why hasn't He done something for you and Dad?"

The father tried to stand in faith, but health problems took their toll on him. His body could not withstand all the stress caused by the court battles concerning the lawsuits, taxes, and creditors. With all the nervousness and worry, his body began to lose function. His mind became confused.

The court battles had lasted for seven years. The attorney fees were more than he could ever pay. All the judgments the creditors had against him had interest and they were continuously pulling him in and out of court for depositions to discover assets he and his wife might have.

Finally, his attorney told him that he could settle with the tax people, and they would discount the penalties, principal, and interest. However, it had to be a cash settlement. The attorney went on to tell him that the judgments filed against him and the business would be on file for seven years, but the creditors could keep them alive for 21 years. The attorney also told him that the courts would force him into settling the lawsuit with the dead man's family.

The attorney said," Why don't we just throw in the towel and quit? I am tired. You and your family have done more than most. Why don't you just take some time, you and your wife pray about it, and see what you want to do." And another thing, the attorney said," My bill is paid in full. You don't owe me anything. As a matter of fact I owe you. The way you just kept on keeping on. Most people would have quit the first six months. We have been fighting for seven years. I am just tired."

The businessman went home in his ten year old car. Looking down at the odometer it had 150,000 miles on it. He began talking to his car saying, " We have been a lot of places together, haven't we? You have been faithful to me and you have been a good car."

A question kept rolling around in his head. " God," he said, " I have trusted You. I did everything I knew to do, but I don't know what to do now. What went wrong in my life?"

The Lord immediately flashed before him his son in rebellion and not serving God - doing things he should not be doing. The son would not listen to anything his father had to say. The Lord spoke to the businessman and said, " Son, look at the way you lived your life against your parents. Did you listen to your father and your mother? Did you?"

Tears started pouring down his eyes. The Lord continued," Son, I have a promise for you and I told you to trust Me. When you honor your father and your mother you will be blessed and have a long life on planet earth."

" Son, all of your life you wanted your father's love and acceptance. But he had his own needs. He couldn't love himself let alone you and your mother. He wanted to love you. He just didn't know how to love you. You rebelled because of the hurt and anger in your heart. Then you cut your parents off. The minute you had the opportunity to leave home you were gone. Money, money, money was your goal. When you got married, your wife was the best thing that ever happened to you. The love you needed as a young man from your mother and father, you could draw out of your wife. Your wife just loved you back, but still you were a driven man. You were driven to succeed and become somebody."

" The reason you wanted to become someone was to show your dad that you're a somebody, a successful businessman. The rejection you held toward your father and your mother tied you to them. Your umbilical cord has not been severed from them. You have not been set free from them to be blessed. Your wife was set free when she got married to you. She could cleave to you, but you could not cleave to her the way you needed to because you never left home. Sure you left home physically, but in the spirit you were tied to them. When you do not honor your parents, it will not go well with you. Your life will be shortened, and your children will cut you off just like you cut your parents off. How many times have you seen your parents? How many times have your children? Do you understand what will happen to your grandchildren. They will be seen by you and your wife just about as much as your parents have seen your children."

" Another thing, son, you judged your father when you

were young. Your grandfather was a successful businessman, and he left your father the business. When the depression came, your father was too young to run the business. He lost it and you judged him as a failure. Do you see when you judged your father, that judgment came on you and now your son is judging you?"

This man broke into a million pieces crying and shaking. The Holy Spirit was showing him all the hurts and pain his father had received during his life.

The Lord said, "Your mom and dad would never spend a penny." You made a vow when you judged your father that you would never be like him and do without. Son, the same time you judged your father is the exact same age the enemy had access into your life. I want to tell you something. If the enemy has an inch he will take a mile. Do you realize as long as your god was mammon, you had all kinds of money? You were in his territory and you bowed the knee to him. You served him. You were ruled by him. When you no longer loved that master, you hated him. You became the enemy. You went against him. When you choose to serve Me, you had a number on your head. The enemy set up every hit man to destroy you, but you are still standing. Trust Me and I will deliver you and set you free. Go to your natural father and forgive him."

That night he went home and told his wife what the Lord had spoken to him. About that time his son came in and sat down on the couch. His father went over to him and sat down and said, " Son, I would like to go see my dad and your grandma. How would you like to take a few days off and drive up to see them?"

The first reaction was very negative, " No, Dad, I don't have the time," his son said. The father was persistent. After several minutes the son asked when they were leaving. The father smiled from ear to ear and told him that they ought to leave at midnight tomorrow.

The next night around 11:30 the son was at the house ready to go. His mother had made plenty of snacks, sandwiches, hot tea and coffee. When all was packed, the father and son were off to grandma's house. The trip was a good twelve hours, so they thought they could surprise the grandparents by showing up at around lunchtime. On the way up the father and son had a great conversation and were able to share their hearts.

At 12:05 they pulled into the driveway of the old farm house. Grandma came to the window and looked out and knew it was her son. When grandpa saw his son and grandson, he quickly grabbed his cane and started to hobble toward them. Tears began to swell in his eyes and the eyes of his son. The grandson bit his lower lip when he saw his father crying. Grandma kept saying, go on in the house, dinner is about ready. Grandma made the best homemade biscuits in the world. The fried chicken was perfect and the gravy was excellent. Questions and answers went back and forth. Before you knew it, tears had turned to laughter. After dinner mom gave them the best piece of apple pie you have ever eaten. The coffee was a special blend and the taste was great. The whole afternoon was great.

Grandpa started talking about old times and said, " I was so dumb in my younger years. I lost a lot of money in business. Oh, if I could live those years over son. I would be a lot wiser in making decisions. I wish I could have spent more time with you, but those years just flew by so quickly. I really don't know where they went, son. I worked on this farm and grew old. When you and your sister left, I didn't really miss you until I lost you. Then I realized how much I really loved you."

The words *I really love you* penetrated the heart of this businessman and set him free to receive the love of his father. Seeing his grandfather and dad love on each caused the grandson's heart to be touched in a way it had never been before.

Grandpa said, " Son, all I ever wanted was for you to be blessed, so you could live a life better than we did. When you left I knew you had to make a living and I knew it would be tough. When you married your wife, I knew she was a good one. I knew you were busy and I just believed one day I could let you know how proud I am to call you my son and to have a grandson as nice as this."

The grandfather reached into his pocket and pulled out an old pocket knife. He took his grandson by the hand and gave him the pocket knife saying," My grandfather gave me this knife and I would like for you to have it."

The grandson wrapped his arms around his grandfather and hugged him and his dad at the same time. The day had past and it was time for bed. Mom had all the beds ready and everyone turned in. The next morning everyone woke up to the smell of biscuits and gravy, eggs, bacon, and coffee. When breakfast was over, Grandpa told them that he would like to take them for a drive.

The three of them got into the old pick-up and bounced through the pasture down to the hay fields. Grandpa started speaking, " Someday son, this will be yours. I would like for you to keep it. My father left me this farm and if it hadn't been for the farm I don't think we would have made it. When I lost the business I wasn't sure what I could do or wanted to do. We came to the farm and lived here. I was so full of fear, I went to work and did anything I could to keep my mind off of my failure."

" The arguments we had in your teen years were not over you, son. They were arguments within myself. It took me years to forgive myself of my failure. My dad worked so hard and gave me a prosperous business. I wasn't prepared to take on the responsibility of running a business. The depression hit and I got wiped out. I had a secretary and an office manager that stole a lot of money from me."

When he said that, the son knew his life was a carbon copy of his father's. The son said, " Dad, what did you do?"

"Well, son," the father said, " It was horrible. Many times all I wanted to do was run away. When I came to the farm, I figured I'd ran far enough - no big cities, no problems with people. I had a lot of time to sort things out. When you kids were young I would take any odd job just to stay busy and make enough money to pay the bills. The years passed pretty quickly. I was scared to do anything. A lot of my friends went broke during the depression and I was scared to take on any debt."

" What got all my friends and me in trouble was the debt we had. I could have made a lot of money buying neighbor-hood farms when they came for sale, but I was scared to take on the debt. I learned to do without. If your mother and I couldn't pay cash for it, we didn't buy it. Today the whole world has gone crazy on debt. Since World War II our country went crazy on buy now and pay later. When you borrow money, son, the only winner is the bank. The banker is always in first place."

"I have seen a lot. I wish I could have shared my life with you, so I could have taught you what not to do in life rather than tell you what to do. Son, life passes pretty quickly. The most important things are your family and the relationship with your Maker. When you become my age, things and money mean nothing. All your mom and I have will go to you and your sister. I hope you keep it and let the grandchildren enjoy it. Your sister has no children, so I left your children an inheritance. Remember, son, the Bible says in Proverbs 13:22, "A good man leaveth an inheritance to his children's children: and the wealth of the sinner is laid up for the just." "

The next day they had to leave for home. Grandma and Grandpa gave them a kiss and a hug and thanked them for coming. On the way home both the businessman and his son had a peace in their hearts. Their hearts had bonded together working a freshness in their relationship. It was a security found through the knowledge of the past and renewed hope for the future.

Twelve hours later they were home. The minute he walked in the door, his wife gave him a big kiss and said, "I have sure missed the two men in my life. How did it go up there?"

"Mom," the son said, "It was wonderful. Grandma and Grandpa are great. I wish they lived closer so I could see them more often."

The father said to his wife," Honey, I am so glad we went. Dad told me things that have helped me, and now I understand some of the feelings I've been experiencing. I couldn't fully understand why my father chose to live life as he has, but now I have a better understanding of him and myself."

Something in the spirit broke that weekend. The attorney called the next morning to ask him about his decision on the bankruptcy. His reply was very simple," Go ahead, file the papers. It is time for our family to be a family again."

That evening, he told the kids and his wife he was going to quit the fight. Mom and the kids leapt from the table, jumping for joy saying, "Yes, yes, now we can get this monkey off our backs."

Within months the bankruptcy courts had finalized all the necessary paperwork and it was over. The men at the shop had no problem with what he did. The court battle for the man falling to his death was dropped. The wife of this man came to him saying, " I found out that the scaffolding my husband was using was worn out. His own workers refused to work on it. They knew someone was going to get hurt or killed on it. When I heard the truth I came to tell you. The accident was my husband's fault, not yours. The attorney that wanted to sue you didn't want to drop the suit. He had so many personal problems that I felt sorry for him."

" When we bought our house and my husband's pick-up, we bought credit life. When he died, the insurance paid off the mortgage and the note on the pick-up. My husband had also bought a life insurance policy. Since my son was so little when my husband died, I took the life insurance money and bought an annuity which paid me 12% interest tax free. That money has doubled, and it should double again before he is ready to go to college. Although I lost my husband, our son will have a future. I want to thank you and tell you I am really sorry for all the turmoil that stupid attorney has caused you and your family."

Within the same twelve months, an aunt died and left his wife a small inheritance. The tax department finally gave in, accepting the amount of the inheritance as payment in full. The only thing left was the creditors who had filed all the judgments against him for bills he didn't owe. These were the debts left when his manager and secretary charged materials to his company and built apartments and houses.

The manager and the secretary had gotten married and gave their lives to Christ. They had so much guilt over what they had done that they could not forgive themselves. Their pastor told them that they had to go to him, give restitution, and ask for forgiveness. The two of them were scared to death, but still called their old boss to ask if they could come over and talk. At first he was speechless, but when they said they had given their lives to the Lord, he agreed with no reservation. He and his wife had prayed for the two of them everyday since the disaster started years ago.

At the meeting the businessman and his wife allowed the couple to share their hearts. The old manager began by saying, " We are very sorry for what we have done. The Lord started to convict us of our sin toward you and Him. We were allowed to see how terrible our lives had become. The Spirit of God directed us to saving grace through Jesus Christ. When we received Him, we became different people. He has truly turned us around."

" We ask for your forgiveness and desire to pay restitution for what we have done. The properties we have are really yours and we would like to give them back to you."

He reached into his briefcase and pulled out a warranty deed and said, " This deed was prepared by our attorney and we would like for you to take it and forgive us for being so stupid. We know we stole from you to buy the land and material to build them. The properties are in great shape and in one of the best areas of town. Here is a check for $100,000.00. It should cover the interest."

You could imagine the surprise of the old boss and his wife. " Yes, yes, yes," is all they could say, " Yes, we forgive you and thank you for being obedient to the Lord."

The next day the business man called his old attorney and told him what had happened. The attorney could not believe his ears. The business man said, " One other thing, I want to pay back every penny to my creditors."

The attorney kept saying, " You don't owe them. It got wiped out in the bankruptcy."

" I don't care. Get a hold of them because I want to pay them," he insisted.

Several weeks later the attorney called him and gave him the total dollar amount. Within days he was at the attorney's office with a cashiers check for the amount. The attorney said, " I have never seen anyone do this before. You are the first."

Within the year the entire town knew what he had done.

His business was more blessed than ever. His employees all became partners, and he was the richest man in town. He was respected and admired by all.

God told him to just trust Him. Every promise we receive in God's word is ours, but we will go through the wilderness before we enter the promised land. Our faith will always be tested. The way we handle the wilderness will determine if we die in the wilderness or go across the Jordan into the promised land.

Years later his father and mother died. To his amazement his dad had acquired millions of dollars in cash, stocks, and bonds. When this man looked through his father's affairs, he was totally amazed at the accumulation of a lifetime of savings.

In another book called *Any Old Dummy Can Make Money, But It Takes A Wise Man To Keep It* , I show people how to take a dollar and use it. I show what this older gentlemen knew, how to save regularly. Not only did he leave millions to his son, the grandchildren got an inheritance which would help them get started.

Many times I have seen professional people with great income worried sick over their money. I have seen the same thing in every level of income. I don't care how little or how much income people have, they still can be in bondage in the realm of finance. I have counseled people who make $10,000 a year and they feel if I could only make $20,000 a year they would be okay. It won't be an hour later and a person making $20,000 a year would say, " Oh, if I could only make $40,000 a year I would be okay."

I have meet people making $50,000 a year who say, "Oh, if I was making $100,000, I would be okay." The $100,000 a year man or woman would say, " Oh if I could make $250,000 a year, I would be okay." I have spoken to the ones that handled millions and guess what. They would say exactly the same thing, " Oh, Mr. Landers, if I could just make $50 million."

In counseling these people, it doesn't matter how little or how much money they make. I know one thing, if you are born a man like myself, you put your pants on exactly the same way I put my pants on. We both have the same amount of time each day. God has given us a body and a mind, and He can certainly help each one of us if we seek His face with a whole heart.

Here are two reasons we don't prosper financially:

1. We have not been taught properly on finance.
     We have not studied the 2,084 verses in the Bible on finance. No one has taught us about the world's system of debt and their ways.

2. The second thing is you have been taught some good principles, but have ignored them.

I have seen satan trap professionals in schemes. The fastest way to lose money is to get into a ball game you know nothing about. While in Australia I would watch rugby on television. The pastor and his friends knew exactly what was going on in the game, but I did not have a clue. That is how a lot of men and women are in investing money. They get involved in a business that they don't have a clue about.

Most times the first loss in the business is the best loss. I have told many people to get out of their bad investments quickly. Some investments are nothing more than money holes that suck all their money into them. I tell them, "You can handle the loss now, but if you stay in, it will drain you. It will steal your finances, your family, and the possibility for an inheritance to your children. Don't throw good money after bad money."

I have seen it happen over and over. They have fear controlling them. The fear tells them that they can't lose the money they already have invested. Before you know it they have gone to the bank to borrow more money. They hold the belief that if they hold out a little longer and invest a little more, it will turn the corner and begin making money.

Do you see how greed has entered in and all the time the interest clock is ticking? The family, the wife, the husband, and the children suffer so much. Debt lasts for years and the children grow so quickly. Dad wakes up one day and he can't believe that he has become a slave to an investment he knew nothing about. He is on the verge of losing his home and life savings, because the business has been nothing more than a scheme to destroy him and his family.

No matter how much money you make, if expenses are greater than income you cannot continue to live on borrowed money. Sooner or later it must be paid back. Learn to save and live within your means.

Bankers and Business

I have seen a lot of men go stir crazy when they reach the age of 40. They have spent 20 years working for someone else. Let me tell you a story about such a man.

He looks in the mirror and sees he is 30 pounds over weight. His hair is turning gray, and he is not as quick as he use to be. He gets the bright idea of going into business for himself. He tells his wife what he is going to do. Oh, what a mistake. He should have prayed with his wife and got into agreement on this major decision in their lives.

He goes down to the bank to get a loan. The banker tells him that he needs collateral, something to hang his hat on. A lot of people don't understand bankers. They think differently than most people. That is why they have all the money and 97% of the people need to borrow their money. A banker looks at a man's ability to repay a loan. Is he working? Is his wife working? How much is their debt? How much goes out every month, and how much stays home? Can he repay this loan?

Some bankers give money on the security of a job and the income it produces. Some people might be in sales and need money for inventory. A banker knows that. He doesn't want to buy inventory, so he needs some additional collateral to hang his hat on. If the borrower doesn't have the collateral, how about his mom and dad, in–laws or a friend. Does the person know anyone who can act as co–signer to guarantee the repayment of the loan?

Other loans are based strictly on equity positions on real-estate. If your farm is worth $500,000.00 and you want to borrow $100,000.00, any banker would take that loan. Other loans are given strictly on collateral and cash flow. Not only does the banker want collateral, he also wants to make sure you have plenty of cash coming in to pay him back.

In this particular instance, this man is quitting a job which produced income every week. The banker is going to give him a loan on the equity in his residence. The house is about paid for, so the banker feels very comfortable in giving him a working capital loan based upon the prime rate of interest and securing the loan by a mortgage on his home.

The day comes when he quits a secure job and has great expectations of being a very successful businessman. The next day is Saturday, and the banker sets time aside at 10:00 a.m. for this gentlemen and his wife to come and sign the note and mortgage.

What this man did not realize is that he had a wrap around mortgage. The bank saw that this man had a 30 year mortgage which had an interest rate at 6–1/2% , so they took over that mortgage and charged this man 10–3/4% interest on the new loan. Immediately the man is losing money. He didn't have a clue, but the banker just made money on his old loan. The banker told him all you have to do is make one payment to us, and we will take care of the old mortgage. We also need 2% for closing. You must pay the charges for the title insurance and appraisal. Before he knew it $2,700.00 was lost on miscellaneous expenses. These expenses were included into the loan on which he would be paying interest. The payment to the bank was $1,250.00 a month. He still had to pay the insurance payments and the real-estate taxes at the end of the year.

How many of you think his wife was jumping for joy over this great decision? Well, she wasn't. Matter of fact she was furious, madder than a wet hen. The first few months weren't too bad because they had a pocketful of money, and both were spending way too much.

Most businesses lose money the first year. The second year you break even, and the third year you should make a profit. Most new businesses can last about 18 months by robbing Peter to pay Paul. That is exactly what happened here. When the second year rolled around, all the cash was gone. Bills were everywhere. They had cancellations on their car and home insurance. The real-estate taxes had been sold to a tax buyer for nonpayment. The bank became upset because checks kept coming in without sufficient funds in the account. So the bank stopped paying them.

The tax buyer notified the bank by certified mail that he was going after a tax deed. The auditors had picked up on the last audit that no insurance was on the autos or home. The payments on the mortgage were late and the bank was sending out certified mail, but it was being returned by the Post Master. The bank also saw that they had been in small claims court on a judgment that was rendered to a supplier for $3,117.97 plus court costs. Taking everything into account, the banker had to call the note and make a demand for full payment.

Friends and Business

That Friday night the two of them decided to go out with friends for dinner. It came time to pay for the meal and he insisted on paying the tab for the four of them. They went to the register to pay and he pulled out his plastic credit card. Within seconds the hostess said, " Sir, you are not valid."

Well, the embarrassment turned him two shades of red. His wife said," Oh, honey, use this one."

Everyone was smiling at each other and the hostess said, " I am really sorry, but this one is not valid either."

The other man then reached into his pocket and paid for the meal with cash. This old friend was one who had worked with him at his previous office. On the way home it wasn't very easy to talk in the car. You could cut the air with a knife. They pulled the car to the curb to drop off their friends. The two of them thanked their friends for the dinner leaving in embarrassment.

Several weeks went by and all the creditors were putting the heat on them. The phone got shut off and the utility companies had sent them disconnect notices. They were so desperate that they started borrowing money from everyone they could. They sold furniture, anything, just to get what? Money. They had to have money. Their thinking was driven every minute of every day. We must get money, money. We must get money.

The friends who had taken them out for dinner called them and wanted to take them out for dinner again. It was their treat. They were very hesitant in accepting, but finally said, okay. The night came and the friends picked them up. At first it was just small talk. As the evening progressed his old friend told him that they were very concerned about their financial affairs and that they wanted to help.

The wife just broke down and the husband had tears rolling down his cheeks. With deep sniffs he cleared his nose and began telling their story to their friends. The wife and confessed that she was so depressed she had gained over 20 pounds in the past several months.

The friend's wife put her arms around her and said, " The reason we asked you to dinner tonight was to see if we could help."

She continued, " I have received a small inheritance from my mother. When she died all her assets were sold and divided equally among my brothers and sisters. My husband and I have talked it over, and we have decided to loan you my inheritance."

When they realized the care their friends had for them, they were elated and humbled at the same time. They looked at each other with joy, then turned to the couple and said,"You don't know how much this means to us. Thank you."

The next week the four of them met. The friends said, "Here is the money we promised to loan you, The terms of repayment are to pay us back as soon as you can."

For several months everything was going great. The bank called them to tell them they would advance an operating loan if someone would sign the note along with them. So they asked their friends and sure enough they agreed to sign the note.

Months flew by and it looked as though everything was going fine. It wasn't. The same old problems popped up again.

They were broke and writing bad checks, robbing Peter to pay Paul. The bank called their friends and said, " You are on the note. You co-signed it and now you must pay."

After talking to the banker, the friend was furious. The quickest way to lose a friendship is to loan a friend money - much less sign a note for him. You guessed it! He had to pay the bank the payment. He became strapped to a monthly payment for the period of four years. The extra financial strain hurt his family and especially his wife. His kids needed things, but there was no money. He was tied to a heavy burden, helping old Pharaoh, the banker, build his pyramid.

The couple lost their friends, their cars, home, and everything. They even lost their marriage. The age of their oldest child? He was 13 years old. The friends who wanted to help got stuck being slaves for four years worth of payments. They lost the only inheritance they would ever receive from her natural parents, and all they wanted to do was help.

I have seen these schemes happen a dozen times over. Why do you think the Bible tells us not to co-sign a note for anyone (Prov.22:26-27)? It says go quickly and cancel what you have done. Don't lose your bed to the creditors. Today we do not have debtor's prison, but if we did, society would be barren and the prisons full.

The first thing this couple should have done was ask their friends what had caused this trouble to begin with. They should have looked at the bills their friends owed and the inventory they had on hand. Never tell a person here is the money and pay me whenever you can. When-you-can never happens. Either put a person on a repayment schedule or just give them the money freely. Think wisely or you may lose a friend and your money.

This woman had an inheritance left to her from her parents. A wise person will leave an inheritance to their children's children. This woman lost hers. The enemy set her up. If you ask this woman and her husband today if they would loan the money, I will bet you a quarter their reply will be no, no way.

When you get a little extra cash the enemy will whisper in your ear, "You don't deserve this money, you didn't earn it. You need to help someone who is in need."

Satan is a counterfeiter. He is the best. You will think it is God talking to you. I have asked numerous couples who have lost their whole life's savings in a deal. I ask them these questions, "Were you and your wife in agreement over the decision? Did your heart tell you to do it, or did your emotions and mind?"

Fear and greed are the two major factors the spirit of mammon will use. Many times the enemy will whisper in our ear to help one person or another, but we think it is God. It was no more God than the man on the moon. It is the enemy. The enemy knows that our hearts are directed toward helping mankind, so when we have a few extra dollars he whispers lies to us. No one has enough money to help everyone. Be selective in who you help. Make sure it is God, and not your own emotions directing you. God would never ask you to loan money blindly. But, He may ask you to give it away. You must find His direction in each circumstance.

Five things to Remember

The first thing you must do is save money weekly, monthly, and yearly. When you make it a habit you will see your money grow. It will secure an inheritance for your children and their children. You will be secure in your older years of life. 97% of the people in the United States go to retirement needing financial help through the government.

The second thing we must learn is to invest the savings wisely, not out of emotions, but out of sound financial planning. When we lose our savings and inheritance, it is gone. The enemy has set these traps for us. We must be wise.

And thirdly, never give your money to someone who seeks to sell a great opportunity, yet rushes you into the investment. Never invest in that nonsense. Invest your money with people that have a track record of making secure investments that make profit, but also are liquid. You may need your principal back for another safe investment. Never spend your principal and interest. When you spend this your multiplication stops.

The fourth thing to remember is to never invest your money in any business you know nothing about. Do not loan your money to any person who thinks he can go into business. Business is tough. The odds of failure are great. All new businesses think they are going to profit. Statistics tell us that most new businesses will not make it past their first year. Most businesses fail because they are under capitalized, and they can't survive the storm. Big business cannot net 10%. If you borrow money and pay interest, look at your expenses and income. It is a tough world out there. I believe the next few years will have more bankruptcies and foreclosures than we have ever seen before. Our debt is too great. Interest will kill you financially.

The fifth and last thing to remember is that most people are very greedy. They will let some friend of a friend talk them into investing their whole life's saving into a project. The people involved will promise to pay huge usury (interest) rates for using the money. Never put your savings into any high risk adventures that promise to pay you huge interest. Most tricksters work on people's greed. Greed will demand us to view an investment by the amount of return alone. Greed demands a great return upon our initial investment, therefore it can blind us to any possible risk. This is the trickster's greatest asset - greed!

In Closing this Chapter

The Lord desires that we prosper. He holds us responsible to prosper. We should seek Him concerning the calling on our life in this area. Instead of running from the responsibility, we should face it squarely. We can look at money, riches, and wealth in a mature fashion. Come to an understanding of the world's system compared to God's system. The servants in the parable were bondservants. They gave their entire life for the service of the master not based on restraint, but because they knew the master loved them. They found security in His service. They were able to partake of the goodness of the master as they multiplied what He placed in their hands. He gives according to our ability and desires that we multiply what He gives.

This is the good news of the Gospel. He preached to the poor so they would be poor no more. He will work on your behalf in the endeavors He gives you to perform. Allow yourself to be blessed with the prosperity God intended for you.

Prayer:

Lord, I renounce the traps of the enemy that have held me in bondage to poverty. Every spirit of poverty must leave me and my family in Jesus name.

I receive the talents You desire that I have to fulfill Your will in my life concerning prosperity.

Lord, please give me the full revelation that I might multiply that which You place in my hands. May I be as Jacob and realize the opportunities You place before me.

Thank You, Lord, for healing the areas of wounding that have come into my life from past mistakes. Help me to stand once again in the place were You have called me to be.

Fill me with Your Spirit of Wisdom so I may leave an inheritance to my children's children in Jesus' name, Amen

Notes

CHAPTER THREE

GENERATIONAL CURSES

Generational Curses

In the 28th chapter of Deuteronomy, we find the curses and blessings of the law. One of the blessings can be found in the eleventh verse. It states, *"And the LORD shall make thee plenteous in goods, in the fruit of thy body, and in the fruit of thy cattle, and in the fruit of thy ground, in the land which the LORD sware unto thy fathers to give thee."*

In the same chapter, a curse is promised to those who will not obey the old ways of wisdom. It states. *"Cursed shall be thy basket and thy store. Cursed shall be the fruit of thy body, and the fruit of thy land, the increase of thy kine, and the flocks of thy sheep. Cursed shalt thou be when thou comest in, and cursed shalt thou be when thou goest out."*

The Lord tells us to choose between the curse or the blessing. Most people can't choose properly between the curse or the blessing because they have been taught principles of life that bring the curse rather than the blessing. How many of you know that it takes more than one option for a choice to exist? The Word says my people perish for the lack of knowledge (Hosea 4:6). If our parents did not teach us properly when we were young, then we must be taught by the Holy Spirit when we are older. God will put His Holy Spirit on the inside of us.

It is a promise, but we must receive Him. It is our choice. God cleanses us when we accept Jesus as Lord and Savior and become born-again. He also wants to fill us with His Spirit of Wisdom so we can make the proper choices in life.

I have noticed through the years that many of the characteristics found in parents are replicated in their children. People will say you are just like your father or just like your mother. You know your son reminds me so much of your father. Our little girl is like her grandmother. The good or bad traits of those in our family can be visited upon us.

EXO. 20:5 *Thou shalt not bow down thyself to them, nor serve them: for I the LORD thy God am a jealous God, visiting the iniquity of the fathers upon the children unto the third and fourth generation of them that hate me;*

If anyone in our family lineage has bowed to serve the teachings of the enemy, those same teachings may be working to bring a curse to our lives. This scripture is a direct reference to our ability to make wealth, our ability to do business and find a place of success in business. If God says that generational curses have the ability to hinder our success, we should desire to deal with those curses directly and permanently.

Through the years I have noticed young teens pregnant or in trouble. When I ask the mother a few questions, something amazing is revealed. Often the mother became pregnant exactly at the same age as the little girl. Looking further back in time we find grandma did the same. The door was wide open for the enemy to attack this young teenage daughter. I have had young women come to me crying their eyes out because their husbands have left them. Many times their mothers have had the exact same thing happen to them. Divorce is a spirit, so if the door is opened into a family, look out.

The same with alcohol, drugs, sex, medical problems, heart attacks, and high blood pressure. Insurance companies consider family health problems as a part of your personal record. If you have not suffered from an ailment, they still consider you a risk if it is prevailing in your family's history. Insurance companies know that certain diseases follow families. Some of these curses are handed down. Read the entire 27th and 28th chapters of Deuteronomy. In these two chapters you will find the blessing and the curse. You will discover that all the diseases plaguing us today are found in the curses.

Generational Curse in Business

Sons follow in their dad's footsteps. I have had many men come to me scared because their grandfather or father died at a young age. Heart attacks, crazy accidents, and things that didn't make sense caused death in the family. I had a father come to me shaking from head to toe. This is his story.

At the age of 57 this man lost a son and a daughter. His eldest son was married and in business doing quite well. He wanted to know if I could take time out of my busy schedule to spend some time with him. When traveling it is very difficult to have any spare time, but I felt drawn to this man. I told him to meet me the next morning.

In the meeting, this gentlemen told me that from the age of 20 he was in business for himself. He got married a few

years later and had several children. He became very successful in business.

He told me that he stood beside the hospital bed of his
father and watched his father die at the age of 76. Tears poured
down his face as he related to me the sadness he felt from the
loss of his father. He couldn't believe how quickly the years
had passed and now his father was gone.

He related to me that at one time his father was a multi-
millionaire. But at the age of 55 he made an investment that
devastated him financially. On the surface the deal seemed to
be a solid one, so the father personally guaranteed the venture. Everything his father had was lost. At the age of 57 the
father went bankrupt without the ability to recover his losses.

He also lost children during that time. The family had to
accept government assistance to survive. His father told him
that his grandfather was very successful and the same things
had happened to him. While his father was lying in the hospital bed ready to die he related that their ancestors had come
from Ireland and their clan had a symbol that was theirs alone.

Remarkably, the man relating his story to me had become a Christian, and he also had bought a business that seemed
to be very prosperous. The accounting books had been twisted
to indicate it was a tremendous cash cow. After the takeover
the cash cow was found to be nothing more than a lame horse.
The horse needed to be shot because it was eating up all the
cash reserves.

As I listened to the history of the family, an amazing fact
was brought to my attention. When the father was in the hos-

pital dying the last words that were spoken to his son were the blessing and the curse of the family. This man was the eldest son and he said a darkness fell upon him at the moment his father died.

The very day of his father's death, the accountants over his businesses called him and expressed great concern regarding the state of his business. The man told them of his father's death and asked them to please wait until after the funeral. His accountants said this problem cannot wait and we must meet with you today.

The man had bought a business that was heavily regulated by the government. The reports that had been sent to the government before the take over were fraudulent reports. His accountants and legal counsel had misadvised him because they had missed the errors. When he signed the legal documents, the sellers were released from any liability and he became the only responsible party. The government had completed their own audit and had found several errors and mistakes on reporting forms. Different accounts in the business had incorrect figures.

His other businesses had equities in them, but all the cash had been taken out of them to buy this business. He bought the business because of its ability to generate a tremendous cash flow.

This man who had just lost his father was in tremendous mourning and at the same time had to deal with the greatest business blunder of his career. He was forced to deal with the accountants. He found that the mistakes were his responsibility and that the fallout was financial destruction.

At the age of 57, his business failed and everything was lost. Between the age of 57 and 59, he lost two of his children. At 59, he needed help from the government to survive like his father. This man had given his life to the Lord, but was still devastated.

The wife had come to the meeting and when I looked into her eyes I could see the depth of pain in her heart. Her heart was broken. She had a wonderful family with many children and a beautiful home she had worked very hard to build. Then disaster hit. This woman with home lost, businesses failed, real- estate relinquished, automobiles repossessed, and worse of all, her children dead felt pitifully hopeless. All the pain and sorrow of these losses were in her eyes.

I also noticed while sitting in the room with them, that they were very sharp to each other. The love they once had was gone. I said to her, " Can I ask you a question?"

She replied, " Why yes, Mr. Landers."

You could tell by her manners that she was a very proper woman. Her composure was wonderful. I asked her," Did your father approve of your marriage?"

With that question her countenance dropped."Mr. Landers," she said, " No, my father never did. You see my father saw my husband and his family as second class. At the time of our marriage my father–in–law to be had to live off of the government. My father would never accept my marriage into such a family."

I then addressed the same question to the husband. I heard

an amazing thing. The answer was the same. His mother and father thought the very same thing. They told him that he was not good enough to marry into such a successful family. Isn't that amazing. One family thought they weren't good enough, and the other family thought they were too good. So, I then asked them about the wedding. Well, you guessed it. It did not go well. Both of them were determined to win the in–laws, but it never worked.

The father–in–law was always upset because the son–in–law kept his little girl bare foot and pregnant. His parents thought the daughter-in-law drove their son into being a work–a–holic so she could have material things. This wasn't the case at all.

At one time this couple really loved one another, but to-day in that office, they were together but a million miles apart. I asked the wife this question, " Do you trust your husband?"

The question broke her heart. She said, " No, I blame my husband for losing our home and my position in life. The only person I really trust is my father. My father told me it would end up this way. We would be penniless and living on relief. Thank God my father is helping take care of us!"

When she said this the husband fell to the floor weeping and crying hysterically. She started screaming so loudly I thought the windows would break. This lasted for several min-utes, and then it seemed as if it was over. Then out of no where the two of them started all over again. This time it was worse.

The Holy Spirit spoke to me and said," Take authority over this tormenting spirit."

I commanded the spirit saying," You tormenting spirit leave them in Jesus' name!"

The minute I commanded that tormenting spirit to leave them, the two of them fell to the floor as if they were dead. I loosened the power of the Holy Spirit to heal them and to let the peace of God fill them.

I had a luncheon engagement, so I left them there on the floor and went to lunch. After my lunch, I went back to the room because I had forgotten my briefcase. When I entered the room, I could not believe my eyes. The two of them were in the exact same spot. They had not moved. They had been on the floor for at least two hours. Reaching for my briefcase, I heard them moving, so I sat down. God was at work. I saw them helping each other up in a love that I knew was real. The moment they stood to their feet, their eyes met each other. They started laughing so hard I couldn't believe my ears. The laugh was not a natural laugh. It was a laugh God had given both of them. I decided I would just sit there and watch what God was doing. They laughed for twenty or thirty minutes. I started laughing because they were laughing. It was good, like a medicine, for all of us.

I prayed over that couple and broke the curse off their remaining children. Through this experience I was able to see the importance of our words. Life and death are in the power of the tongue. Mothers and fathers can bless their children or curse their children with the words that roll off their tongues.

Later that week, this man asked me out for an evening meal after the financial seminar I was doing. (I learned the hard way that I never eat before a meeting.) I told them that the only way I would go with them was if I could pay for their meal. This man's wife said, " Mr. Landers, please come."

I told them I would meet them by the door at the north exit. I had to get my coat, hat, and briefcase. Have you ever had a debate with the Lord? Well, I did. The Lord told me, " Ray, listen to me. I want to set this couple free. If they ask you one more time to pay for your dinner, you let them!"

Here I am saying, " Lord, they don't have the money. Let me buy, I want to buy them their meal."

The Lord said, " That's just it. You are able to, but they need to be set free. They are so scared. Fear has overtaken both of them. They will always be in poverty if they don't change. I am telling you right now, I want you to pray over this couple."

Everything the Lord was giving me was in supersonic speed. I said, " Lord, will you slow down? I can't think this fast."

The Lord told me that the Irish symbol was a demonic symbol over this family. Great, great, great-grandpa had made an oath to the enemy. In the oath he promised his eldest son to the enemy. The Lord told me that the man who made the oath was very selfish and would not honor Him, but chose the ways of the enemy instead. The oath opened the door for the enemy to destroy the first born son's finances, his children, and in the end, his life.

The Lord said, " Tonight I am setting them free. After they buy your meal, you must tell them that the money they just planted into your ministry was by My direction. Because they were obedient, I am going to break the spirit of fear and the spirit of poverty off of them. If the two of them will stay united in agreement, the curse will be broken and I am going to walk them through this. Tell them I am in control now, not satan."

When God finished speaking to me, my knees were knocking and I said," Okay, Lord, I will obey you fully in everything tonight. I won't offer to buy their dinner."

I'll always remember this discourse with God because I remember saying, " But God, all I wanted to do was buy them dinner."

I had to realize God's ways are higher than my ways. He has spiritual reasons for the things He does, and many times they are tied to our obedience in the natural realm. If He wanted to break a spirit of poverty from these precious people by having them minister to me in the midst of their need, I was not going to hinder His plan.

I met them at the door and the smile and twinkle in their eyes reflected the joy of God in their hearts. The husband said, " Mr. Landers, I have been visiting with my uncle for a couple days, he shared some interesting things with me."

I said ," Oh really, what might that be."

The man said, " My uncle said that his father and grand-father were very happy that they had been born the second and third sons."

This really interested me. I couldn't wait to hear more, "Tell me about this!"

He continued," My uncle is very successful in life and as many generations as he could trace, we have been very prominent people. All my aunts and uncles have prospered in every generation."

"My uncle also told me how his father was told by his grandfather that the original man making the oath did it to bless himself and his family. He did not want his family nor their descendants to go through life in poverty. So he invoked the oath to bless all of his children except the firstborn son. He sacrificed his firstborn son for the rest of the family, so all the other children could be blessed. My uncle said he saw his own brother, my father, become very successful only to end in poverty."

Continuing he said, " After receiving this information, I went through my father's possessions. I found the family seal that was given to him by my grandfather. When his father gave him the seal he made him swear to give it to his firstborn son and in turn told him to hand it down to his first born-son. My father on his death bed made me swear to give it to my firstborn son. My father told me I must do it for our family's name to be blessed."

As I sat there listening, I shook my head in disbelief. Yet, I believed every word this man said to me.

I was so mad I thought I could not control the anger rising up through me. My mind was going crazy. My guts were jumping up and down so fast that I had to grab the arm of the chair with all my strength just to control myself. I was praying so hard that I don't know if I was praying out-loud or to myself. I could hear the Lord as clearly as a bell telling me what to do. He was giving me specific instructions for the destruction of this thing. God showed me the symbol which brought death and destruction to the firstborn son for all of these generations.

God said, " I gave My Son to redeem his children from the curses of the enemy, and this night the destruction stops for this family."

The wife, sensing my intensity, very quickly took the bill and said," Mr. Landers, please let me buy. I have been hiding this money and I would be honored to buy your dinner," I thanked her.

On the way home I told them what the Lord had showed me. I told them that everything they had told me was a complete confirmation right down to their uncle's report. While we were eating dinner, they showed me the family seal. When I saw it, the Lord instructed me to tell them to melt the seal to liquid form just like Moses instructed Aaron concerning the golden calf. I told them once they melt it down to throw into a river or lake.

I instructed them exactly the way the Lord had shown me. I then prayed for all the generational curses over them to be broken. We accepted the blood of the Lamb, God's firstborn Son, as the sacrifice for this family and claimed God's prosperity for all their generations.

In this story, the Lord told me, " Son, just because you are born-again and filled with the Holy Spirit, don't think for one minute the enemy doesn't have access to you."

Dear brothers and sisters, any legal right the enemy sees to bring destruction to you and your family is an open door he will walk through. He comes to kill, steal, and destroy our families. If we don't know our covenant rights in Christ Jesus, the enemy will take advantage of our ignorance. Jesus died for the whole world, but only those who appropriate salvation receive salvation. It is the same with freedom from the curses of the law. You might be saved and on your way to heaven, but unless you appropriate freedom from the curses, the enemy will seek to stay in the ground he believes is his and will take any ground you give him legal right to occupy. We must understand the enemy's schemes so we can fully cover ourselves.

What drives me crazy is that in many churches it is said, " Oh, don't worry about that. It is under the Blood."

Brothers and sisters, it is not automatic. You may be a father who never drank a drop of alcohol, but in your parents' lineage someone had a terrible problem and was considered a drunk. Perhaps your child becomes an alcoholic. The enemy is very deceptive and patient in his attacks. In this type of situation, he will set you up to reject your child based upon your ability to refrain from the abuse of alcohol.

What if your great-grandfather was the one who had the alcohol problem? Most likely the family will not remember his problem. The curse caused by the great-grandfather can reach to the forth generation. In this instance your grandson could carry the same problem as the great-grandfather.

Satan uses time as one of his greatest tools in the destruction of people through generational curses. He may skip one or more generations when setting up an attack. His purpose is to mislead us into judging the person rather than dealing with the source of the problem. He uses time as a tool to disconnect us from the spiritual truth of his involvement. He also desires to cover the tracks that lead to the open door.

For instance, if no one in your immediate family has misused alcohol, there would be no reference point in dealing with the problem. If suddenly a youth within the family begins heavy use, the whole family could point a finger of accusation toward the youth. Yet, the problem could be an attack based on a generational curse. The family wouldn't know to break the curse because they didn't realize one existed. Thus, the enemy has succeeded in his scheme. This principle works in every area of life, not just alcoholism.

Some of the worst secrets of our forefathers find their way into the hearts of our children. The enemy wants us to believe we cannot relate to the problems that face us, therefore we become powerless to do anything about them.

God gave us a book called the Bible. If we don't train up our children in the way they should go, guess what! We can't yell and scream at them. We trained them. We wrestle not against flesh and blood. Our fight is not with what they are doing, but with what causes them to do what they are doing. Setting them free from the curses of the law is a part of our responsibility as a parent. In doing so, we will be training them to overcome the attacks of the evil one.

God has given us an awesome responsibility as parents to train our children. We must train them about the things of God in life including finances. Let us fulfill the responsibility wisely as good stewards of the greatest treasures on this planet, *the hearts of our children*!

The Generational Curse of Debt

DEUT. 28:12 *The LORD shall open unto thee his good treasure, the heaven to give the rain unto thy land in his season, and to bless all the work of thine hand: and thou shalt lend unto many nations, and thou shalt not borrow.*

One of the greatest blessings in the scriptures can be found in Due 28:12. It states that God desires His people to be lenders rather than borrowers. In the book *Kings and Priest over the Financial Realm* I speak in deeper detail concerning the ability to become a lender rather than a borrower. But in keeping within the scope of this book, we will only look at the principles concerning mammon and debt.

Almost everyone within our society is bound by the spirit of mammon. The desire to own possessions consumes their every moment. They work to have a place to lay their heads, but that place must be respectable enough to relate the image they desire to those around them. Jesus said the gentiles worry about what to wear and how they will live, but you should not be concerned about these things. Seek first the kingdom of God and these things will be added to you.

He was telling us to first seek the authority of God's rulership in these matters, and things would be added. He does not desire to withhold material possessions from us, but He does desire that we receive them without the spirit of mammon attaching himself to them. If we do it His way, we find great freedom to prosper.

When we have not been blessed by an earthly father through godly instruction and relationship, the curses passed to him are passed to us. The true image of who we are can become distorted. We can believe that our self-worth is measured by the things we own rather than by the person we are. When this is the basis for our life, a door opens for the spirit of mammon to attack us. We feel a strong temptation to build an illusion of self-worth through the use of debt. The desire to build this illusion can be a generational curse that consumes our income so we will not be able to acquire wealth.

Credit, on the other hand, gives us a false sense of prosperity. We think we can own a house or a car and spend to the limit of the credit offered to us. Many young people are up to their ears in debt. They try to look successful in society because they do not have the proper foundation within the Word of God to protect them and guide them into true wealth.

Most of the church has followed this same pattern of debt based living. To be a borrower is a part of the curse not a part of the blessing. The blessing states that we will be the lenders and not the borrowers, the head and not the tail. We must awaken to the fact that we have become slaves to this world system of finance. It is bleeding the funds from the church through the debt of her people.

The fear of God is the beginning of all wisdom. We must first believe what He says before we can receive the wisdom to gain the wealth He desires us to make. We can become debt-free and teach our children the same blessing. If we train our children to get the plastic charge card out instead of paying cash, the children will be trained to be a slave to the lender. They will learn at a young age to become borrowers.

Our lives and the lives of our future generations do not need to be consumed by the servicing of debts that God never intended for us to have. I am aware of the difficulties that arise from being a borrower, and I am aware of the difficulty in believing that we can be lenders. I know the questions going through your mind as you read this particular section of this book. But you must believe that the truth of the Word of God can set you free.

The Spirit of Mammon and Debt

The spirit of mammon can find ground through a generational curse. The desire to spend for the pleasure of spending can be passed from one generation to another. Those of us who use credit to buy goods or treasures as a means to fulfill a sense of loss in personal relationships could be depending upon things rather than upon God. Although it may be something taught to us by others, we are still allowing things to bring comfort to our hearts, rather than a relationship with God. This is one principle the teachings of Jesus relates to us when He warned against a dependency upon things for our happiness.

The spirit of mammon wants to come into our lives in times of personal depression. It desires to give us a sense of euphoria, a high, in order to addict us to spending. He will use past and present injury as an avenue to push us into a buying spree. Some of us have been taught by our parents to spend for a sense of power over another individual. When our lives are out of control, spending can give us a sense of power and control. These actions are being directed by a spirit of mammon.

Mammon wants us to have a need to spend because it uses credit and debt to enslave us. If we are not healed from past wounds or from the generational curses in our life, mammon has an open door to enslave us through the debt we create.

Many have lost their lives through the misuse of credit. They buy to fulfill a personal need and use credit rather than cash. It doesn't take long for debt to become such a deep hole that it is impossible for them to escape. The walls cave in around them and they become buried in the debt they've created. At this point many marriages end in divorce because they were standing on a false foundation of credit. Men kill themselves rather than face the personal humiliation of being known as a failure.

Jabez Breaks the Pattern

(1 Chronicles 4:9-10) In the times of old names were meaningful. A name could be either a curse or a blessing. For Jabez it was the curse. His name was given to him by his mother and it meant sorrow. Sorrow means, mental suffering or pain caused by injury, loss or despair. It also means worry and heaviness caused by grief. Jabez had a very strong curse placed on him at the inception of his life. He was known as the one who causes sorrow.

All of us who have been cursed by our parents can fully relate to Jabez. No matter how hard we try it is impossible to please everyone. Sometimes everything we do is simply not good enough. We feel as though we live in the proverbial doghouse. Trouble seems to follow us wherever we go, while peace of mind escapes us. The feeling of unworthiness and perpetual lack rather than blessing can become the norm. This way of life can find its root in a parental curse.

Jabez was named by his mother at his birth. This has significance because it relates back to the original curse placed on child bearing after the fall in the garden. Eve was to bear children through multiplied sorrow and pain (Gen. 2:16). When Jabez's mother gave him his name, she was binding him to the original curse.

Blessing was also spoken to the women concerning child bearing. The blessing was related in the words spoken to the serpent when God said, *"And I will put enmity between thee and the woman, and between thy seed and her seed; it shall bruise thy head, and thou shalt bruise his heel."* (GEN. 3:15) In this scripture God promised man the ability to rise above the tactics of the enemy. The foot of man striking the head of the serpent places man above the enemy, not below him. The mother of Jabez chose the curse for her son. Every time Jabez's name was called, it was establishing the curse over his life rather than the blessing.

Many of us have been bound to the curse through the words of our parents. Phrases such as, you will never amount to anything, and you're just like your uncle Bob! You will turn out just as bad as he did! You are nothing but a loser! The list goes on and on. The words spoken over some of us could not appear in a secular publication much less a Christian one.

When we are young, the opinions of our parents are very important to us. What they say has tremendous power to shape us into the individual God intended us to become. However, if the words spoken are from the curse, they have power to destroy our true potential. Words spoken from the curse create a negative image, and through this image we picture ourselves as the person we are told we are and become blinded to the person God has made us to be. Some of us are still controlled by the words spoken to us at a very young age. They are of the curse, and the curse can be broken.

Jabez sought God with his whole heart for freedom from the curse placed upon him. Here is his prayer found in 1CH 4:10 *"And Jabez called on the God of Israel, saying, Oh that thou wouldest bless me indeed, and enlarge my coast, and that thine hand might be with me, and that thou wouldest keep me from evil, that it may not grieve me! And God granted him that which he requested."*

The first thing he asked was for the blessing to overtake the curse. The blessings of God are always stronger than any curse. But we must appropriate the blessing in order to break the curse of the parent. Parents have spiritual authority delegated to them to either bless us or curse us.

The second was for his boundaries to be enlarged. He was asking for a larger vision. He no longer desired to see things from the vantage point of the curse. He had felt the sting of the curse operating in his life, so he desired to view things from the point of the blessing. He knew if he could break the curse the boundaries in his life could be overcome.

He knew he could reach a higher level of living, spiritually and materially.

Thirdly, he sought God to work on his behalf. He placed everything into the hands of God. He desired godliness to rule over his heart, so he might be a blessing. He wanted his identity to be found in God's opinion of him not the curse nor man's opinion. He wanted the supernatural power of God to help him on a daily basis.

Finally, Jabez requested safety from evil. He wanted freedom from the reputation the curse had given him. He desired release from the fear of loss, caused by his past sins and bad decisions. His request was granted, because Jabez asked God to be the source of his blessing. Jabez believed that God's love was greater than the power of any curse. Because Jabez asked, God gave him freedom from his personal curse. God wants to do the same for you.

Jabez lived in Old Testament times. We now live in New Testament times. Jesus has redeemed us from the curse of the law (Gal. 3:13). We must be as Jabez and appropriate what God has given. We must rise above our earthly generational curses and receive the total freedom that comes through Jesus Christ our redeemer.

Again I would like to lead you in prayer. This time let's pray concerning any generational curses that may have found their way into your life.

Prayer:

Dear Father, I ask that You would reveal to me any generational curse that has come into my family lineage. Help me find the total freedom You desire for me and my family.

I renounce and sever myself from all generational curses that have come from my mother's or my father's line, in Jesus' name.

I renounce any curse that has come through any spoken word or unholy action. All curses must fall to the ground and find no place of power within my life and the life of my loved ones.

I rebuke every unholy spirit that is not of the Spirit of God from my home and my life in Jesus name. You must leave my children and me, in Jesus name.

Lord, please heal me from the words spoken by my mother or my father that have caused me to see myself in a way that is not healthy. Please restore to me a proper image of who I am in Your wonderful Grace.

Please give me the grace to receive the truth of Your blessing so I can become a lender and not a borrower in Jesus' name.

Please fill each area with Your Spirit and uphold me with Your loving, Fatherly hand. I thank you in Jesus' name.

Notes

CHAPTER FOUR

THE SPIRIT OF MAMMON

The Spirit of Mammon

This final chapter deals specifically with mammon as a spirit. Mammon is a spiritual force that influences everyone directly or indirectly, in the church or out of the church, Christian or unbeliever. This spirit has no economic nor ethnic boundaries. Every human being will be tested by this spirit. Therefore, my desire is for you to be able to easily recognize the characteristics and signs of mammon in your life and in the lives of those around you. In the previous chapters, we have separated wealth from mammon, and we have told you stories about the effects of mammon on others. Now, in this final chapter, we will look at mammon as a spirit. We will describe its characteristics and the warning signs of its influence upon your life.

Characteristics of Mammon

There are six characteristics that describe the spirit of mammon:

I. Its foundation is iniquity.

The spirit of mammon is a driving force that consumes the lives of men and women in their quest for money. It will pervert love and cause us to care for things or possessions over people and God. It will drive people to steal, kill, and destroy human life and dignity.

All of us have heard numerous stories about a husband or a wife killing their spouse for the insurance or inheritance money. What about grandchildren killing their grand parents, children killing their parents, uncles and aunts, brothers and sisters, all killing one another for one thing - money!!

The foundation of love is broken into small pieces and carried away by a lust for money.

When the spirit of mammon enters the framework of a person's life, they will view people as objects to be used rather than treasures to be loved. Why do drug dealers deal drugs, and why do prostitutes prostitute? Why do large companies down size? The bottom line is all the same, it's for the money.

The spirit of mammon tells us we are not worthy of re-spect without attaining the full benefits of the society we live in. Therefore, we become preoccupied with the acquisition of things rather than true love. Mom and dad have to work to keep up with the Jones'. The newer home and the sportier car are all paid for by the lives of our neglected children. Many children are buried in the foundation of our workaholism and become lost to us forever.

II. It is anti-God.

The spirit of mammon is a hunter of human souls. It wants our mind, our emotions and our will to be so entangled within the natural things of this world that we forget God. Its sole purpose is to capture us in a scheme and destroy us. For some of us this spirit wants to create a place of perpetual lack, but for others, it wants to give a sense of false security through the use of earthly riches. Both are extremes that dishonor God.

This spirit wants to lead us into a place of self-reliance, so our dependency will be on ourselves and the things we can accomplish, rather than relationship with God. The spirit of mammon will generate a sense of pride in ourselves and our abilities, so we will deny the need for the presence of God.

III. It is a little thing.

The spirit of mammon is a little spirit that demands great attention. It wants us to believe that it has great authority over our lives. The spirit of mammon wants us to believe that our whole life is dependent on it, rather than dependent upon God. It makes money, treasures, and earthly riches seem more important than they really are. *What does it profit a man if he gains the whole world, but looses his own soul?* (Mat. 16:26)?

The spirit of mammon wants to deceive us by telling us that we are powerless to stand against it. Yet, the name of Jesus is above every name in heaven and earth, and mammon must bow to that name. Nothing, is greater than the Lord we serve. Mammon must, and will, fall like all the rest.

IV. It is a liar.

The spirit of mammon finds its power through the lies it

tells, and its authority over us is found in the lies we believe. The lies this spirit tells seem like reality. This present system of finances and marketing is fertile ground for the spirit of mammon to take root and flourish. We need money to operate business. We need money to operate the church. Wherever money exists, there is the spirit of mammon seeking to tempt.

This spirit will always seek to secure its authority over the system it has helped to create. The system of mammon permeates every nation of the earth, and all of mankind is running the rat race it has created for them. No wonder the lies it tells seem to be focused in reality. It is reality for most of the world, but not for the Christian.

Only the truth about this present system sets us free from mammon's deadly effects. We must watch over our minds with diligence, because money and this present marketing system are continually bombarding them with their agenda. Their desire is for our lives to be consumed with nonessentials, so we can be drawn away and lose faith in God.

V. It gives limited enjoyment.

The possessions and pleasures of this present system of mammon give enjoyment for a limited season. How many of us have been caught up in this trap? The spirit of mammon says to us. "Oh, if you could just get a new home you would be happy."
Then it says,"Your car isn't as nice as your neighbors, you should go buy a new one."
Then it says, "You need a new job."

This spirit will speak to men and women in a specific way according to their need. For women the answer is: new clothes, jewelry, makeup, or a perm. Mammon will tell men they need: new tools, a snowmobile, a jet ski, or a new boat. At times, we will buy anything that will temporarily comfort our souls. Yet, when we get the things we believe we want, the flare of excitement burns for a brief moment.

When the soul is out of peace, the flesh with the spirit of mammon will work overtime to comfort it. Oh, go get drunk, go have an affair, go, go, go. The devil will use anything to bring enjoyment to you *for a season*.

VI. Its home is in another kingdom.

God does not use the spirit of mammon to comfort us. That is satan's work. All the characteristics of mammon are opposite of God's ways. The god of this world's system has blinded the minds of those who find their home in his system. (II Cor. 4:4).

In the world's system, everything is done through buying and selling. If you hand someone money, you expect something in return. If you don't receive a good, a service, or a product you feel cheated. How many of you have bought something at one store only to find it at a lower price in another store? What do you feel when this happens? Many people will take the merchandise back to the first store and tell them a story to get their money back. Then will they go to the other store and purchase the same item at a lower price. Why will many stores sell you merchandise for the price you can find it somewhere else? Because they want to keep your business in their store.

The Kingdom of God operates in a way that is opposite of this world's system. Everything in God's Kingdom is done through giving and receiving. Freely you have received, so freely you give (Matt. 10:8). In God's Kingdom there are no personal attachments to things, therefore, there is no selfishness or greed. In God's Kingdom, He owns everything and gives it freely to whom He wills. I speak about this in greater detail in my book, *Kings and Priests over the Financial Realm.*

These six characteristics of the spirit of mammon only touch briefly on the true character of its existence. There is much more to learn when considering this spiritual force and it's function as an emissary of satan upon the peoples of the world. This spirit will have a major role at the end of the age. It will take part in the strong delusion that will separate men from God for eternity (II Thes.2:11).

Nevertheless, we must move on to the signs that reveal its influence on our individual lives.

◆ Worry over finances.

Worry over the financial realm is a deep seated fear that there will not be enough money to meet all the obligations. This sign is a clear indication that a spirit of mammon has held hands with the spirit of debt to attack our life. Mammon leads us into a need to buy, while the spirit of debt gives us false hope for the future. When our debt becomes larger than our income, worry finds a place of authority to rule our hearts. Mismanaged income will always lead to worry, and the spirits of debt and mammon will always be around to help us into greater troubles.

Borrowing money is not wrong if it is used properly. When you use debt to create wealth you are using God's wisdom and your assets will increase. But, when you use credit to buy depreciable merchandise, you will eventually become a slave to debt. You will come under the curse of being a borrower and never a lender.

Credit card companies are the largest tool in the enemy's hands when it comes to enslaving people to debt. In the Old Testament the Jewish people could not charge a brother usury (interest) on the money they would lend (Duet.23:19-20). Whenever you borrow money with interest attached to it, you become a slave to the lender.

In Proverbs 22:7 it states: *The rich ruleth over the poor, and the borrower is servant to the lender.*

The word for servant in this scripture means bondservant or one that is in bondage. Interest will cause the lender and borrower to enter into a master slave relationship. Once a slave it is nearly impossible to find freedom outside the grace of God. Month after month and year after year that same old debt is still there, although you have paid the principle back double or triple. In these situations two-thirds of our lives are eaten away through the servicing of debt. Two-thirds of what could have been ours becomes someone else's just for the luxury of credit.

Before you use that credit card, ask yourself a question, " Do I really need this?"

Just because the card is plastic, don't think your not deal-ing with money. You will have to pay it back with interest.

♦   Can't afford it.

One of the greatest tools of the enemy is the *I can't af-ford it* syndrome. Many people say, " Me tithe? I can't afford it!" Non-tithers in the body of Christ are doomed to debt. They are sitting targets for the spirit of mammon and debt. They take themselves out of the protection God has promised to all tithers. If you feel that you cannot tithe, you are already a slave to this present world's system. The best thing you can do is ask God for forgiveness and begin to tithe this week.

♦   Impulsive buying.

Look around your home, in your closets, on your shelves, in your cabinets, in your garage, in your storage areas, in the trunk of your car. What do you find? Do your find things that you bought on sale, yet never use? You could be an impulsive buyer, and the spirit of mammon might be influencing your decisions. Do you buy things because you think you will save money, but never use them? No one saves money through im-pulsive buying, but they do save money by placing it in a bank or a retirement fund and leaving it alone.

Those who have bought something through the desire to buy rather than through the need of the object were under the spell of mammon.

♦ **Discontentment.**

The spirit of mammon wants our souls to be out of peace, therefore he speaks to us through discontentment. Those suffering from this attack cannot find happiness in anything. They will be unhappy about their spouse, unhappy about their children, unhappy about their home, unhappy about their car, unhappy about their job. All of these things could change, but they would still be unhappy. Give thanks for this is the will of God concerning you. Also contentment with Godliness is great gain.

♦ **Stinginess.**

A stingy person cannot give freely without attachment to the gift. They believe anything given must have a return. They cannot receive gifts graciously from others even if they where freely given. This causes complications in their minds. They begin to think, " If they gave me a gift I must buy them one in return. If I buy them one in return others will see it. Then I will have to buy everyone a gift. I wish this person would have kept their stupid gift. This gift is really going to cost me."
Such people are bound by the spirit of mammon.

♦ **Bondage to debt.**

Most people are bound to debt without knowing it. I ask them the question, " Do you own your own home?"

" Oh yes, Mr. Landers, we do," is the normal reply.

I ask, " Is it paid for?"

" Oh, Mr. Landers, you can never get your home paid for. We have a thirty-year mortgage that we just refinanced. Our payments have went down one hundred and eighty dollars a month. Isn't that great, Mr. Landers?" they state smiling.

I ask, " By the way, do you own your furniture?"

" Yes we do, Mr. Landers," they reply.

" Do you owe anything on the furniture?" I ask.

They reply, " Yes we do, but we don't have any interest on all our new furniture for one full year. We also put new carpet and tile throughout the entire house and we have no payment for six full months."

" What's the interest rate on the carpet?" I ask.

" Mr. Landers, it's really cheap. It's only 1-1/2% per month," they reply. (One and one-half multiplied by twelve equals 18% per year. That is not cheap!)

Then I ask them, "What about your clothes and appliances such as your stove, refrigerator, television, and stereo?"

" Well, Mr. Landers, those are on our credit cards: Sears, Montgomery Wards, Visa, plus a few others. But it's all right, because the payments amount to only a few hundred dollars a month. Our television is one of those big screen televisions. It only cost us a couple thousand dollars. We're buying it from one of those electronic stores where you pay weekly, but we really enjoy having the television. Our clothes are ours, but we pay on our credit cards monthly for them."

I ask another question," Do you own the vehicles that you drive?"

They reply," Oh yes, Mr. Landers, we do. GMAC had this 2.9% finance charge on their new cars, so we bought two new ones. They are very nice and we really love our cars. We pay for them with our second check each month."

I then ask, " Do you both work?"

They reply with, " Yes, yes we do."

I ask, " Does it take both of your salaries to make ends meet?"

" Yes, it does," they say.

" What type of tools do you have in your garage?" I ask.

" Mr. Landers, we have our own riding lawn mower, hedge trimmers, and all the tools we need. There is a wonderful business man in our church. He owns an implement dealership, plus he is so nice, He gives us anything we need and tells us to pay him as soon as we can," was the answer.

I say to myself that this situation is not nice. I can see the hand writing on the wall. They are open game for the devil. He has an open door straight into their lives, and through them he can cause great distress within the church. The spirit of mammon is setting them up for a fall. In the process, the businessman will be injured and confusion will enter the church.

Not one thing these people thought they owned was their own. They were living in a false sense of security that would eventually be toppled by the spirit of mammon and debt. They were in bondage, but thought they were prosperous. One mis-step would send them into a tailspin that could destroy their fantasy life-style. One loss of a job, one sickness, or one accident would destroy their whole system of management. They were one step away from bankruptcy with a blindfold tied around their eyes.

Bondage to debt comes slowly, but its effects can last a lifetime.

◆   **Fear and greed.**

Thoughts of fear and greed are developed by listening to the spirit of mammon and are projected upon the screen of our imagination as we focus on them as truth. Fear and greed are not just words, but they are imaginations and feelings. The spirit of mammon binds itself to us with the cords of fear and greed.

Fear is a crippler. It breaks our ability to think through faith. Faith will always lead us with peace of heart and will bring forth a positive outcome. Fear, on the other hand, causes us to be double-minded and unable to make a wise decision. When a choice is made through fear, it is usually the wrong one.

Fear can also be demanding. It wants to rush us into action before an action should be taken. It wants to push us into situations without the counsel of God. Many examples could be told, because fear can grip so many different areas of our lives. Yet in keeping our reference to mammon and its power to persuade us, let's look at an example that describes the fear of loss. A person goes into an apartment store to do a little shopping. They see something on sale. Because they don't really need it, they are hesitant to buy it. Then along comes a salesman and tells the person, " This is the best sale on this particular item that we have ever had. By the way, this one is the very last one in the store."

Within the heart of the shopper the spirit of fear manifests itself as a sense of loss. Fear of loss can truly bind us to a sale. It is one of the greatest tools of any salesman. Many car salesman, appliance salesman, and even Realtors use this ploy to boost their sales. Some salesman will lie to you and tell you two or three other people are also interested in the same item, just to move you to buy. In this instance, the need for the product as the motivation for buying is superseded by the fear of loosing it to someone else. It may not be a deal, but many times the fear of loss is a very strong persuader.

On the other hand, the fear of loss can manifest itself in a fashion entirely the opposite of what was just mentioned. The fear of loss could cause the same person to be indecisive when investing in a somewhat secure, yet profitable venture. Fear of loss can hinder someone from making a correct career move, or even from taking the step into marriage.

Lets compare the different types of fear with greed. Fear of failure causes us to bury our talents in the ground of disbelief. On the other hand, greed causes us to covet that which belong to another. Fear of loss can make us too timid to take the next step, being compared to greed as an opportunist waiting to take advantage of someone else's misfortune.

Greed causes money to control us, rather than our controlling money. When greed is in a person's life, money makes that person a slave and the desire for money rules over their actions. But when a person makes money their slave and begins to rule over it, then the spirit of mammon will be broken from their life. A sure sign of this accomplishment is when the person begins giving into the Kingdom of God instead of spending all their resources and time building their own kingdom.

◆ A poverty mentality.

Many believe that poverty only has to do with the poor, but that is simple not true. Jesus said that the poor would always be with us. What we are talking about is a spirit of poverty that can attack the poor as well as those with great material holdings.

Many older people in our society today were very young during the days of the Great Depression. During their childhood, a spirit of poverty attached itself to their thinking. They can have a million dollars in the bank, but are so controlled by mammon that they cannot spend a dime of their money. They will absolutely deprive themselves of food, clothes, and the bare necessities of life, because the fear of the past dictates their present.

Fear and greed control their thoughts on a daily basis.

They won't buy a meal out, and when someone invites them out for a meal, they will become upset as they watch others spend money to enjoy themselves. They would rather starve than spend five dollars on a meal, so they tell everyone that they are not hungry. When a child or adult doesn't finish everything on their plate, sometimes this person will gather all the food from each plate and eat it. They believe the old saying, "Nothing should go to waste!"

When they get older they can't enjoy anything. Tears pour from their eyes because they believe that their children will spend their money foolishly.

The Depression created a whole generation of these people. Being controlled by the fear of death, they are scared over the possibility of loss. They are unable to live a normal life. This is all the product of the spirit of mammon releasing the spirit of poverty on mankind during a very dark era of our history. The Depression caused many suicides and the destruction of many families. The enemy used the fear of the future to destroy many people.

Many in our generation have had the same mentality of poverty passed to them through their family linage. Here are some of the signs that indicate a spirit of poverty influencing a daily life and the future prosperity of a person.

When they go out to eat they save the scraps and the left overs. They are the ones who take the small packages of ketchup and mustard home. They take the salt and pepper packets, the napkins, and the cream. They would take every packet if they could.

Everything they get they save. Newspapers or magazines can be found stacked on tables and chairs or pushed into closets or drawers. Every plastic sack is saved. Plastic bottles, aluminium cans, empty cereal boxes, old clothes, and old shoes are all kept because someday they may be of use.

Their drawers are full of coupons that are years out of date and old bills are stuffed away, although they where paid years ago. They have an inability to open a drawer because of the things that are in it. They need to move things they use on a daily basis to a lower drawer in the dresser, because the other drawers have become full of things they can't throw away, yet never use. Their clothes are stacked on top of the dresser because there is no room in the dresser. There are boxes full of things stacked behind chairs or under desks and tables.

When a person is unable to throw anything away, it is a sure sign that a poverty mentality is controlling them through the spirit of mammon.

Before our closing prayer, I would like for you to examine your life. Look at the lives of your parents and grandparents to find any possible influence they may have had in your life or in the lives of those in your family. These are ways that have dishonored God and His ways. Then let's go back to the third and fourth generations and confess the sins of our forefathers concerning the spirit of mammon and its effects on us and our future generations.

It is time to stand up and fight the enemy on the ground that Jesus has prepared for us. Jesus has leveled the battlefield and has given us superior weapons to win the battle. It is time that we stop laying our armor aside by using the excuse that all is under the blood. Jesus shed His blood to purchase the weapons of our warfare, and by leading captivity captive He gave gifts to men. He has placed the sword of the Spirit into our hands that we may be victors over the wiles of the deceiver. We are not ignorant concerning the ways of the enemy, so let us move forward with a heart full of the battle cry of the Lord of Host and soundly defeat the accuser and thief. Let's drive him far from the territory God has promised to all those who by faith would fight the good fight of faith and conquer the land placed before them.

Prayer:

As we pray this final prayer let's make it a personal prayer, one from our heart directly to God's heart. Speak it out loud and let the power of God bless and encourage you. Let the enemy feel the rebuke of a Mighty God as you take the authority God has given you over the wicked one. Let us pray:

Father, in the name of Jesus Christ of Nazereth, I bind the strong man in the spirit realm. By Your grace I loosen Your anointing to destroy the yokes of bondages that have held me in the enemy's camp.

Jesus, cleanse my mind and make it free from worry. Set me free from the spirit of mammon and every influence that has come to me from my forefathers. Please forgive me for every act that I have performed under its influence in my life.

Strengthen me, Lord, to resist the life-styles I've learned from the spirit of mammon. Satan, I tell you to get your hands off of my household and my children and their children in Jesus' name. Get your hands off of everything concerning me.

I plead the Blood of the Lamb over every door that has been opened into my life through the sins and iniquities of my forefathers.

I take authority over fear and greed and I command them to leave my life. Spirit of mammon and every other spirit under its influence, you must loose your hold upon my life. You must leave me in Jesus' name.

Jesus, thank You for Your Wisdom. Please fill me with Your Spirit of Wisdom in the places where the enemy has had influence.

Father, I thank you that You have heard my cries and You have delivered me into Your wonderful Kingdom, through the precious blood of Your dear Son.

Now Father God, let Your face shine upon me and give me peace in every area of my life, spirit, soul, and body, Thank you Jesus and glory to God.

Ten useful Principles For Kingdom Living

1. Buy things for their usefulness rather than for status.

We should never buy homes, cars, jewelry, clothes, or anything for status. Let me tell you a short story.

I had a friend who did real-estate appraisals for a living. One day he told me a story about a very large home in an elite country club subdivision.

The owner of the house had a BMW and his wife drove a Mercedes-Benz. The man and his wife wore expensive clothing and jewelry.

Looking at the outside of the house, the grass was beautifully manicured and the landscaping was perfect. But, there was only one thing that was odd. The drapes were pulled shut over every window except the living room. The living room faced the front of the house and was easily visible from the road.

Entering the home, my friend noticed the living room was full of very cheap furniture, which had the appearance of very expensive furnishings.

As he did the appraisal, he went around in the home doing his usual measuring and writing down each room's dimensions. To his amazement there was no furniture in any of the other rooms, except the master bedroom. There he found only a boxspring and mattress sitting on the floor.

My friend struck up a conversation with the owners and he asked them if they were just moving in. They looked surprised at the question, but answered it anyway. They told my friend they had been living in the home for three years and needed the appraisal to refinance their home.

From the outside this couple looked like they were a part of the yippie group-young and making a lot of money. In reality they owned nothing and were living in a false world. As we say in the Midwestern United States, "All show, but no go."

Many people in the world try to live a false image, just to impress their neighbors. They will go deep into debt and enter a master slave relationship with old Pharaoh, the banker. So many times this relationship only ends in bankruptcy, and the person pays a heavy price in their spirit, soul and body.

Never try to live in a false life-style. Live within your means.

2. Refuse anything that is producing an addiction in you.

Many people hide themselves in their work. Workaholics are the same as alcoholics, only the motives are different. Both separate us from our families. The bondage to debt has been one of the major factors in the creation of workaholics. Never allow work or anything else to come before your relationship with God and your family.

The enemy can enslave us in many different areas: drugs, alcohol, sex, greed, gluttony, and a false image of ourselves. We must put God first in our lives to escape each bondage.

Seek God first and He will heal you and set you free so all good things may be added to you.

Be patient and allow God to bring the increase.

3. Develop a habit of giving; De-accumulate.

Plainly look at the things you have that are accumulating in your home and garage. If you're not using them, give them away. Give, give, give - give it away. When you give freely, God can credit your heavenly account.

When we give, the spirit of mammon is broken off of our lives and we place ourselves in the position of becoming receivers.

4. Refuse to be patronized by the custodians of modern gadgetry.

New HiFi VCRs, televisions, C.D.'s, computers, and all sorts of electrical devices seek to lure us into a spending spree which we cannot afford.

This holiday season I went to several electronic stores and could hardly believe my eyes. I had not seen so much money being spent in all my life.

One manager told me that the day after Thanksgiving, they sold five hundred thousand dollars worth of electrical equipment in one day. I could not fathom a half-million dollars spent in one store in one day.

Be very wise in the purchasing of this type of equipment. Be especially careful if you are using credit cards or delayed payment plans.

Interest on credit cards can enslave you for many, many years.

5. Learn to enjoy things without owning them.

In my travels, I have meet some of the most precious people on God's green earth. Mark 10:29-30 tells us that when we leave our mothers and our fathers, our sisters and our brothers, our lands and our homes, we will receive a hundredfold return in this lifetime, with persecution.

Many other's like myself are walking testimonies to that verse of scripture. I've stayed in people's homes, eaten at their tables, and slept in their beds. I have enjoyed their accommodations and have shared their joys and their sorrows. It is no accident when we meet people. It is a divine appointment. God puts it together.

We can't own everything. Such an attitude is great bondage. Have a could-take-it-or-leave-it attitude. There are too many things out there to be bought. Enjoy other's having nice things, too. Be happy for them, even if they are strangers to you.

It is a sad thing to have the desire to own everything you like. My wife took some friends to an old clock store. One friend bought a clock she wanted to give to one of our daughters for Christmas. It was a most unusual clock, but he saw it first. I'm glad we can enjoy others having what we ourselves want.

Enjoy your life. Share your possessions. Give and receive. When you hold on to something too tightly, you will most likely lose it. You may keep it for a season or possibly a life-time, but your second or third generation will most likely lose it.

Never let anything own you and you don't have to own everything.

6. Develop a deeper appreciation for God's creation.

Many people I see are slaves to a master. They are so far in debt they can't think in a straight line. They hate their jobs. They are stuck in a rut and can't get out. They can't smell the roses. Most of them go to bed at night tired and wake up the next morning more exhausted than the day before.

Learn to give God first place in your life and secondly, give time to your loved ones. Take some walks through the parks. Go out into the timbers and listen to the wind blowing through the trees. Listen to the birds singing and the water flowing through the streams. Get up before the sun comes up and watch the darkness fade away into a beautiful morning. Watch a sunset and the moon and stars come out in the evening.

Learn to appreciate God's creation.

7. Watch the buy now, pay later syndrome.

The retailers and wholesalers of the world will give you a 100% guarantee when you buy their products. If you are not fully satisfied, they will refund your money with no questions asked.

Walmart has become the retailer of America through standing by their products and guarantees. Big businesses know that if they can get their merchandise into the hands of the public, the increase of their sales will multiply by the hundreds.

The first thing a car dealer wants you to do is get behind the wheel of their car. They tell you what a great deal the price is. They quickly let you know they have buy now easy payment plans.

If you pay in cash or know the money is going out of your checking now, it makes a difference in your amount of spending. I can keep a $100 dollar bill in my wallet for a longer time than lesser bills. The plastic card seems like nothing to wave through the machines.

You can even buy now and pay later for a pack of gum with a credit card. There seems to be no reason to hold back when you can have it *now*.

Watch out for , "Buy now, and pay later."

8. Use plan honest speech.

One of the biggest problems in the church is that many people are afraid of telling the truth. Instead of looking honestly at their needs and problems, they seek to confess the opposite. They cannot be transparent enough to receive true healing.

There is a lie that has been propagated within the church. It states that if you speak the truth about your situation, the enemy has an open door to attack you through the confession of your own mouth. If your situation is caused by the enemy, then he has already attacked you. Telling the right people can bring healing.

Confess your faults one to another that you may be healed (James 5:16). Make sure you confess your fault to a righteous person (someone with the tenderness and wisdom to help you), one who loves and cares for you, rather than a religious person who will only judge you.

Another problem within the church is when the leadership asks a member of the body to help serve in some kind of capacity. When the normal response of a person is, "Well, let me pray about it." That person knows they aren't going to help. Why not be honest and just say no.

Be honest to God and those around you. Let your yes be yes, and your no be no.

9. Reject anything that would breed opposition from others, or that is at the expense of others.

While living in the Midwest, I've seen a lot of changes in agriculture. The older farmers have retired and moved off the farms. Several have died and the land has been sold. In the past, the farms were rented for fifty/fifty rent. In other words, the owner of the land would make fifty percent of the increase of the crop, while the one renting it, would also receive fifty percent. But, today most of the agreements have changed to cash rent.

I remember one tenant farmer who got himself into a lot of trouble by using other tenant farmers as stepping stones for his own agenda. He went to the landlords in the area and offered them large cash rents for their farms. This took the farms away from the other tenant farmers, and some of them had farmed the acreage twenty, twenty-five, and thirty years. Several of these tenants hated this individual, because they had to leave the farm and find work in the city. Others were old enough to retire, so they moved into the local town.

I've lived long enough to know what comes around goes around. This farmer prospered for a season, you could see him at the local farm implement company as he bought new machinery. You could also see him at the local auto dealership buying new trucks and cars, all with new telephones installed. He was really wheeling and dealing.

Seed-time to harvest is God's law; not man's. The seeds he had planted through the actions of his life came back on his head. The hurt and pain he had caused others was now returning to him. He bit off more than he could chew, and he paid dearly. I won't go into all the details, but today he has no farms or machinery and he is not farming.

Don't think for one minute that you will prosper at the expense of someone else. When you hurt someone else for your financial gain, your day is coming. It may be one day, one year, or thirty years, but you will eventually pay dearly.

10. Shun whatever would distract you from your main goal... Seeking first the Kingdom of God and His Righteousness.

The devil will get you into all kinds of good works. We can be consumed by our job or even the desire to be a good parent. There are never enough hours in the day to get everything done.

We must take time daily for our relationship with God. We must give Him first place. We have all tried to do things our own way, but what do we really accomplish? Let's give Him the place of honor He deserves.

God promised us length of days in our right hand and wealth and riches in our left hand (Proverbs 3:16). How much plainer can that statement be? Seek His Kingdom first, and all these things shall be added to you.

A Short Synopsis

Just as there are rules of the road when driving a vehicle,

there are rules to attaining wealth. Both sets of rules, if not followed, can cause lifelong injury or death. Here is a brief road lesson on your way down the road to wealth.

Make money your slave. Make it work for you and never devour its offspring. Let its children multiply and work for you. Never let money possess you. You are its master and not its servant. You are created in the image of God. Never bow your knee as a servant to money. Keep your integrity.

Allow God's guidance in your life. Believe in and follow the inner voice of God's Spirit when seeking to purchase anything. If you don't have inner peace, wait. I have a friend who was looking into buying a computer. He saw one that he liked and had a great desire to buy it. But the inner voice of God told him to wait.

A year later, he was prompted to go to the same store and look at the same computer. He ended the transaction with the manager of the store, and instead of leaving the store with one computer, he left with three computers. The price he paid for the three computers was less than the price he was willing to pay a year earlier for the one computer. Ask God for His wisdom when handling money. Wisdom is the ability to make a decision today which will enrich you tomorrow.

Learn God's wisdom in handling wealth. Wealth will always increase, and as it increases it can generate more money. Money will allow you to buy riches so you may increase your holdings in this present system of finance. Always remember where you came from, and who has blessed you.

When riches increase so does the temptation to depend

on them. The temptation to view yourself as a self-made man will be echoed by those who will then surround you. The pride of life will seek to destroy the foundation of your faith.

Learn to give things away freely, because God has freely given to you the greatest treasure that man could ever receive, eternal life. When giving becomes a natural part of your life it will center you in the truth of receiving. You will always be able to rest in the security of God's protection over everything He has placed into your hands. Your view will not be set on ownership of possessions, but you become focused on the fact that you are a good steward of the goods the Lord has given into your trust. Someday He will return and say, "Well done, good and faithful servant, enter into My rest."

Personal Testimony

My life was consumed by the spirit of mammon. I didn't realize that fact until God gave me the revelation concerning the two masters found in Mat. 6:24.

My life from very early childhood was influenced in the discovery of buying and selling. Everything I heard and everything I did was centered around thoughts of money. On the farm we raised cattle and hogs. We grew corn and soy beans, wheat and straw, clover and alfalfa hay. Everything we did dealt with money.

My mother taught me well. She taught me the art of making a deal. Her instructions included the ability to listen so I could say the right things to the right people to get the best price for the most profit. She taught me the art of negotiation for the purpose of transacting a settlement that would always be in my favor. In the process, the same spirit that was on my parents began to control me.

I could never spend a dollar without sensing guilt. If my spending did not include a profit, I felt that I was wasting money, and wasting money was a sin. One of the hardest things for me to do was going out after a basketball game and buying a hamburger and soda. It was a chore to go to a movie on a Friday or Saturday night with Billie Sue. The sin for me was not going to the movie, but I felt sinful because of the money I would have to spent to get in the theater and buy the popcorn and drinks. I hated to spend money. I was controlled by the spirit of mammon.

I remember at a very young age, I would confess that someday I'm going to be a millionaire. My thoughts were always on increase. I loved to buy and sell to make money. It was my thrill in life!

When I married Billie Sue, I had a job at a local fertilizer plant. I had gone into the Air-Force National Guard during the Viet-Nam War, so I had to spend one weekend a month at the Springfield Airport, too. I soon had a second job as a fireman there working the late shift. It was nothing for me to work eighty to one hundred hours a week at my two jobs.

Billie was going to college and it took a lot of money for her to finish her degrees. During those years, I began investing in real-estate. I will never forget coming home one day all excited because I had just bought a farm. The price I paid was four-hundred thousand dollars, but I was going to make a very large profit on the resale of the property.

My wife needed to go to the store that evening to buy groceries and the children needed shoes. I went too and will never forget that night because of what happened. I had around three-hundred dollars in my wallet. Billie Sue needed my cash for the things she was purchasing. I immediately broke out in a cold sweat and my stomach began to churn. I spoke some very harsh words to Billie and wounded her heart.

Here I had just spent four-hundred thousand dollars to buy a farm, and Billie Sue spent less than three-hundred dollars on household expenses. I couldn't handle the guilt of giving her the money, nor the spirit that reacted to her in such a terrible way.

I knew it wasn't my normal personality, but the evil feeling had absolutely consumed me. On the way home I felt horrible. Billie didn't say a word to me. I had a lot of time to think.

At that time in my life, I had no idea what was taking place inside of me. I knew something had a grip on me and I wanted to be free. I just didn't know what it was or how to deal with it.

My wife later told me that she would have panic attacks in the grocery store, or any other place where she had to spend more than a few dollars. The same spirit that was upon me began to attack her.

Today, years later, I can openly confess that God in His great mercy has revealed the truth concerning this powerful spirit. My wife and I are so grateful to be free. I can invite others out to eat and find pleasure in their company as I pick up the check. I used to hate Christmas because of the presents I felt I had to buy. Now I love watching my loved ones open the gifts I picked out. I even grocery shop for my wife! I find as much pleasure in giving as I do in receiving.

As I travel around the world teaching my financial seminars, I teach from my life's experiences, I teach the things God has revealed to me for my deliverance and restoration. All of us need help in the midst of our troubles. That is why He gave us one another.

I hope this book has enlightened you and blessed you. I pray a rich reward on each of you in the days to follow.

God bless all of you!

Ray F. Landers

Notes